SHE
IS
SAFE

SHE
IS
SAFE

STORIES OF RESILIENCE AND HOPE
FROM THE WELLHOUSE

Union Hill Publishing
200 Union Hill Drive, Suite 200
Birmingham, AL 35209

www.richardesimmons3.com

1 2 3 4 5 6 7 8 9 10

Printed in the United States of America

TABLE OF CONTENTS

FOREWORD

I WAS FIRST INTRODUCED to the atrocity of human trafficking while working with the GAL Program in South Carolina. Then, my knowledge deepened as I led the Alabama CASA Network. In each of these roles, the shameless practice of families trafficking their children for money, food, shelter, or drugs brought me to my knees as I sought to understand what really cannot be understood. And it now had a name—familial trafficking.

Soon after attending a National CASA Conference where I participated in a heart-wrenching workshop on the trafficking of children, I sought out a speaker on human trafficking for our State's CASA Conference. I learned that a very short distance from my home existed a ministry, founded by a survivor who was working with such victims – The WellHouse. I also began to learn that human trafficking is not exclusive to families trafficking children, but also happens many other ways when someone chooses to use force, fraud, or coercion to enslave another for their own selfish purposes.

Then, my journey began as I accepted the offer to serve as Executive Director at The WellHouse. Walking the road of healing with each of the survivors and overcomers of sex trafficking featured in this book has been among the greatest privileges of my life. Deep, personal pains in my own life have equipped me to better be able to serve at The Well-House. Even through God-ordained and God-allowed pain, I have experienced purpose in this ministry that has allowed me to find meaning even in the fiercest trials of spiritual warfare.

God has allowed the enemy to use very heavy artillery against many of us serving at The WellHouse, and many times, as I wondered why, awareness of the great purpose of our work meant the enemy was forcefully attempting to destroy those carrying out the greatest purpose. If successful, that purpose would be destroyed.

But Scripture invites us to endure and persevere through trials and pain. I often tell the survivors who make their way to The WellHouse that they are way ahead of most, because they have endured and survived what most of us do not even know exists. The stories they carry display a fortitude and perseverance that leads me to believe that they are among the most prized people, especially to God. I have long admired them and have deeply valued that I have been allowed to be a part of their lives. Much like the women in scripture who suffered greatly (Tamar, Bathsheba, Rahab, Mary Magdalene), these overcomers of human sex trafficking are clearly very special to Jesus! And, ministering to them has brought great joy and healing to my own heart.

Throughout the stories in this book, told in survivors' own words, a clear pattern emerges that is the same pattern around which programming was built at The WellHouse. It includes a painful childhood, not of their choosing, that brought a vulnerability to trafficking and often drug use, and finally, a path to healing through faith in a true and living God. Their deliverance is ongoing, but they are now able to enjoy their lives as they experience their purpose.

Still, there are so many more who we long to see recovered and offered the same opportunities. But God is not finished! We can to look forward to more miraculous stories of the fulfillment of God's purpose in lives once thought hopeless. And I personally look forward to an eternity of fellowship with these very special women.

I could not write these words without acknowledging and thanking many who have walked alongside women on this journey. They include, but are not limited to: our incredibly heroic staff at The WellHouse, our Board of Directors, our volunteers, and our faithful donors, including: individuals, churches, businesses, and foundations. Thank you so very much on behalf of the hundreds who have experienced healing at The WellHouse! May these stories bless you and inspire you to continue this great work.

Carolyn Potter
Chief Executive Officer of The WellHouse

"Fairy tales are more than true—not because they tell us dragons exist, but because they tell us dragons can be beaten."

—GK Chesterton, paraphrased by Neil Gaiman

INTRODUCTION

*T*HESE ARE NOT FAIRYTALES. They are true accounts from women who have walked among dragons. They are true stories of human beings who were bought and sold as commodities to be used and then discarded. As you read each short story, you will find the chains of addiction, abuse, trauma, grief, and lost childhoods are heavy.

You may find yourself asking: how much weight can the human soul bear? How much stress can the body endure? How dark is the shadow of death in this valley of dry bones?

But as you persevere in reading each woman's story, you will find that God is moving and working in unlikely places. The Holy One, who reigns over all creation and sits enthroned in the presence of angels, is also present among the contrite and lowly. How much can the soul & body endure? We need not look further than to Jesus Christ himself, who bore the weight of all sin in his body and soul on the cross. And like these women, He has emerged whole and victorious, setting captives free in his restorative wake, and slaying the dragons of death and darkness.

Are you ready to see the beauty and heights of a life restored? First, we must go low like He did.

TRIGGER WARNING

Some readers may find the content of this book disturbing. These stories are not written for young readers. We would also like to issue a trigger warning for any survivors of abuse, trauma, or human-trafficking.

ABOUT OUR PROCESS

Each story in this book is a true story, even though the names, places, and identifying details may have been altered to protect the identities of survivors and any pending litigation. Each story was written with the assistance of a writing team who took great care in listening to the story of each survivor in a sensitive manner that did not cause re-traumatization. Each survivor was compensated for their time in telling their story.

The writing team includes:
· Holly Bunn
· Debby Haralson
· Paul Lawler
· Carolyn Potter
· Amber Tolbert

ABOUT PROCEEDS

Proceeds from this book will be used to benefit The Well-House. Each survivor and writing team member chose to participate to benefit the amazing work of The WellHouse. We thank you for your contribution to this ministry.

MATTIE

He will wipe away every tear from their eyes, and death shall be no more, neither shall there be mourning, nor crying, nor pain anymore, for the former things have passed away. And he who was seated on the throne said, "Behold, I am making all things new."

–*Revelation 21:4-5*

G asoline dripped from my naked body as I stood near the gas station pump. I shook, because when he doused me with gasoline, I had a lit cigarette in my mouth.

All I wanted was to call my mom. I was finally ready but had avoided calling her for so long. I hadn't wanted the questions or the shame. But I didn't have her number. He did. And he had my phone. Anyone who had helped me thus far only got me into deeper trouble. Who could I turn to?

So, I just shook, not only afraid of a blaze, but of the gaze of the onlookers surveilling my exposed skin, dripping with fuel, the fumes stinging my nostrils. And hope seemed as far away as that Kentucky summer before I became a teenager.

I spent a lot of time that summer in a minivan with my dad and brothers. The sticky Appalachian air was unrelenting at times. The open windows and doors of our van didn't shield us from the stifling Kentucky heat with no air conditioning. I probably barely noticed the summertime perfume of the weeds around the place I lived my whole life. Small city, big town they called it.

We had moved into a trailer. It was in the middle of nowhere, but my brothers and I got to share the spare room. I took care of my brothers when they were babies, but as we got older, we just fought more.

My parents got divorced and our home life was a constant cycle of screaming, yelling, police, and court hearings. I became rebellious and turned to boys for attention and affection.

When I was 16 years old I got pregnant.

I had feelings for a guy I connected with online. At school, he was one of those guys that all the girls wanted to date. If he noticed you, then you knew you were pretty, that you were cool, that you mattered. And I fell hard for him.

I ran into him at the mall one night and he invited me over to hangout with him and his friends. I had to sneak out of the house to go meet him. I told him that I didn't want to do anything sexual, but then the sweet-talking and the pressure started. I had only been with one person before that.

Afterward, I got up to leave and walked out his door.

The greens of summer and the reds of autumn had long passed. The hills of Kentucky were covered by thick snow and it took me an hour and a half to walk home, crunching through the ice on the side of the road. Alone.

My one night stand left me feeling lonely. I started self-harming as I became bullied at school. When I realized that I had not had my period in a while, I walked into a clinic near my school. The doctor confirmed my parents' worst fears with two thin blue lines. They were so mad. Oh my Lord, they were angry.

A family member told me I should just get rid of it by taking the morning after pill. But, I knew I was already 6 weeks pregnant. And for me, abortion was not an option I wanted to consider. That family member did not want me to ruin my future, but I told myself that I didn't have much of a future going any way.

When I called my child's father, he didn't initially want anything to do with the baby. For the first two and a half years of my son's life, his father was not really in the picture. So I had to do it all on my own, even with my continued lack of maturity.

My home life became more unstable, and I went with my baby into foster care. When I aged out of the system, money became tight real quick.

There were four strip clubs in the area. My friend suggested that we try it out. This was not something that fit my personality; it was very intimidating. But we walked up to the windowless building and inside, where they asked us to start working that night. I made $100 on my first night. To me, that was a lot of money. The quick money became addicting. I did not see any problem with it if I was financially stable, holding things together, taking care of my child, taking care of my friends.

But that lifestyle destroyed me.

I lost everything because of the people that I was letting live with me. I had just wanted people to be my friends. I had just wanted someone to be true to me. Money was the only way to get that.

But soon I lost my son in court. I knew I was not in a good place. After I lost my son, I lost control of my whole self. I didn't care any more. I didn't care what happened.

Maybe my son would be better off without me.

I began to spiral downward. I couldn't face my mom or anyone who would only tell me how horrible I was. I just looked for cheap acceptance.

I met a lady at the strip club named Bunny who would disciple me into the lifestyle by taking me under her wing. She had crazy parties at hotels and would let me stay at her house.

The first night that I ended up staying with Bunny, she introduced me to this guy Hatter. They fed me pot and then ecstasy. They continued feeding me drugs, and I kept spiraling deeper down into the rabbit hole. Pretty soon they were feeding me cocaine and acid.

"Come on, just try it."

"Just do it."

I gave in. Even to the meth.

We were reckless, breaking into buildings. He shot his gun into the air in the middle of the city. "Are you scared?" he menacingly teased.

I knew they were purposefully tripping me out.

Is this the fast life? Is this the party life?

It was intimidating, but I was free falling. And somehow I was completely into it. I decided to leave with Bunny and Hatter. They split up these huge stacks of bills, maybe $10k. I had to carry some of the bills in my purse and they had the rest in theirs.

We were on our way down to Dallas. I knew I couldn't dance in the strip clubs because I didn't have my IDs. I felt uneasy when they asked me to give over the rest of the money to Hatter, but Bunny reassured me. I would be taken care of, she said.

They tried to get me to flirt with a guy for a reduced rate. They said I would only need to hang out with the guy, but not do anything sexual. When I walked into the room in my sundress, Bunny lifted up my dress and made me twirl for the guy. I didn't know what to think. Then they asked me to walk the streets. When I made it clear that I was not going to do it, they abandoned me and left for Mexico.

I had about $100 left. Even so, I did not want to call my mom. I knew I would get an earful. I had gotten myself into this mess, so I needed to get myself out.

I stayed in that hotel for days. When I would walk across

the street to the gas station, men would stop their cars to ask if I wanted a ride. I did not even understand that these men were looking for prostitutes.

This girl walked up to me and invited me to come work at the strip club. She said that her boyfriend Chester would come stay at the hotel at night and give rides to the strip club.

The first day, I didn't really make any significant money at the club, but we went to get some fast food. Chester paid for it, which I thought was pretty cool.

When we got up to the hotel room, the door slammed. I heard screaming and yelling. The curtains of the hotel blew open and I could finally see what was going on: trafficking.

He grabbed the girl by the back of the neck and flew her across the hotel room. She was screaming asking me to go get help. I ran down the hallway, but then she popped her head back out and said "never mind come back here... right now."

I wanted to go down and talk to someone at the front desk, but then she threatened to drag me back in by my hair if I didn't go back right then. I was so afraid that I walked back. He started yelling and then took my cell phone to make sure I hadn't called 911. He started choking the girl out in the hallway. He was hurting her and I was begging him to let her go.

A man walks out of his room and asks if there is a problem. I said "Yes. Obviously." But Chester pulled out a gun and pointed it back and forth between me and the guy in the hallway.

"If you really want some problems, we can go back to the back where there are no cameras."

I learned quickly that what happens in the streets stays in the streets. I was desperately hoping for someone to do something, but they lived in fear just like me, not wanting to get shot or beat up. Even the manager at the hotel knew what was going on, but instead he was trying to kick me out because I had allegedly caused the stir in the hallway.

Two young teenage girls came toward my room after seeing what happened in the hallway. They said they saw the man's gun. I told them I was from Kentucky and I just wanted to go home. I thought I might finally have some help. But these girls, their mom, and the guy with them try to get me to sell my body. I could not believe that wherever I turned there was trafficking.

These poor girls were living out of hotel rooms. I thought that they might be able to help me, but they proved that I had nowhere to place my trust. I still think about them and wonder if they are safe...

Still I was just so stubborn. Why wouldn't I just call my mother with all this going down?

Finally when I was doused in gasoline, shamed in front of the onlookers, I realized it was time to call my mom.

I had a different picture in my head of what The WellHouse would look like or what it was really about. I had never been in a program in my life, so I wondered if it was everyone bunking in the same room or if it was like jail. I had never been to jail. But I was so traumatized. I didn't have any options. I was completely broken. On the outside, I seemed beyond help. But my mom, being my mom, saw something inside of me that could be saved or changed. My mom was the one who initially connected me with The WellHouse.

I did the intake on the phone with the Rescue Coordinator, a lady with the most southern accent. I had no clue what this was about.

I got the call from my mom that I had been accepted to The WellHouse. I don't know why all of a sudden I was okay with going, but honestly, I did not want to die. The drugs that were given to me had heroin. I was scared that people would spike my drugs and I would overdose and die.

In September of 2018, I finally arrived at The WellHouse.

I was still high on drugs. I said I hadn't done meth for two weeks, but that was a lie. I had done it that morning. I just didn't want to be judged, although I am sure that they could tell. They made sure that I didn't have any weapons or anything that could harm anyone else.

I felt crazy when I first arrived. Literally crazy. I am pretty sure I annoyed half the girls in that place. At the time, I didn't think I was a drug addict because I could stop using for two or three days. I thought I would only be there for a few weeks and then I would go home. One of the house mothers told me that I wasn't going anywhere. I listened to her. I stayed.

It was a beautiful home. I had already painted a picture in my head, but it was different than I had imagined.

The first few months I bucked the system. I did not like all the rules, classes, and getting up early. It seemed like too much work!

But the people at The WellHouse loved me when I was at my lowest. They loved me until I could love myself. Until I could understand that I deserved a better life. The longer I stayed in the program, the drugs continued to leave my system and I got psychological help through counseling. I began to get well. I began to realize the toll that drugs had taken on my mind.

It was a slow transformation. But I began to bond with the women around me. We discussed all that we had experienced. Through the process, I found out who I was.

Having to face the things people did to me was hard.

Having to face my own actions was hard.

Having to face what I put my mother and son through was hardest. I put them through hell. Facing yourself is the hardest thing you will ever have to do. That was the toughest time of my life, walking through my past sins. But it was freeing. I was able to lay aside those weights of guilt.

I began to let go of the fear and the deep trauma.

I experienced dialectical and cognitive behavior therapy at The WellHouse.

I experienced talk therapy.

The change I experienced from when I first walked into that place was a complete 180, a 100% transformation.

It took me a lot of time and gentleness for me to be free. In fact, I carried a notebook wherever I went that had a full list of my traumatic experiences. Everything that had happened to me. I wrote it all down and obsessed over the weight of trauma that my little notebook carried. It took me a good long time and a lot of therapy sessions to finally put down my trauma book.

And through my mental and physical healing, I met Jesus. I knew about God as a child. My grandfather was a pastor. But I never really had a relationship with God, only knew things about Him. The people at The WellHouse, the volunteers, they loved me more than I could love myself. They loved me with the love of Jesus.

I was there for nearly two years. But I was ready to reunite with my child. I moved back to Kentucky.

I have been able to go to all my court hearings and slowly gain access to more time with my son. He now shares time between me and his dad.

I am currently two and half years sober, and my time at The WellHouse has had a ripple effect on my life. I work at a sober-living maternity house, helping pregnant women who are fighting for their sobriety. A decade ago, I never would have believed that I would be working with mothers in recovery.

But I have this deep empathy for people who are going through a hard season. I went through something similar, crunching through ice on the side of the road in a frigid Kentucky winter and feeling the sting of fear from fumes in the sticky Texas summer heat.

But now, things seem to be falling into place. And it's a new season for me and my son.

It feels like springtime again. ✧

A PART OF OUR PROCESS

CRY FOR HELP. It all starts when we receive a phone call . . .

The Rescue Supervisor will conduct a thorough assessment to determine whether the person is indeed a trafficking survivor and if she is ready to receive the help offered by The WellHouse.

At times, the person calling the crisis line is experiencing a different issue besides trafficking, such as domestic violence or substance abuse. In these cases, the Rescue Supervisor will facilitate a referral to another agency.

If the caller needs to detox from substances, the Rescue Supervisor will initiate this process prior to her coming to The WellHouse.

If there are issues regarding the legal system, agreements are made on the part of The WellHouse to ensure compliance with any agency involved, such as: the judicial system, probation or parole office, and any other necessary entities.

This initial stage of the process helps set the survivor up for success as she navigates the flawed systems that might otherwise hinder her recovery, if she did not have adequate support.

She is just beginning the hard work.

MARTHA

I counsel you to buy from me gold refined by fire, so that you may be rich, and white garments so that you may clothe yourself and the shame of your nakedness may not be seen, and salve to anoint your eyes, so that you may see. Those whom I love, I reprove and discipline, so be zealous and repent. Behold, I stand at the door and knock. If anyone hears my voice and opens the door, I will come in to him and eat with him, and he with me. The one who conquers, I will grant him to sit with me on my throne, as I also conquered and sat down with my Father on his throne.

Revelation 3:18–21

B lue lights pulsed against the bare walls of the small apartment. Very few people knew where I was hiding. As I pulled the curtain back to see what was happening, an entire row of police cars lined the middle of the parking lot. I opened the second-floor apartment door to investigate and made eye contact with one of the police officers.

He scurried up the steps and stood at the threshold of my open door. Looking me straight in the eye he pleaded, "Please go home. Your parents want you to come home." I stood and stared a hole right through him - emotionless. I replied, "I can't go back home."

I had no idea I was the reason all the police were at the apartment. Gripped by fear and shame, I felt paralyzed.

I grew up in Marietta, a city near Atlanta, Georgia. I was born in Honduras and was adopted when I was 18 months old. Growing up as the middle child among five children in an upper-middle-class family, our mom and dad gave us a lot of love and attention. Our home life felt secure and was filled with lots of warm memories. I always felt a deep love for my family.

I attended private school and did well. I cared about my grades and ran track and cross country. I particularly excelled at cross country and started on the high school cross country team while still in middle school. I was active in our home church, participating in weekly worship and in youth group. I had lots of friends and enjoyed spending time with them in social activities and on weekends.

But when I was 15 years old, a guy reached out to me on social media. As we interacted, he invited me to meet him at a public park. Because a public park is out in the open, I felt it was a safe place to meet him and get to know him better. But at the park, he sexually assaulted me.

As a 15-year-old girl, I didn't know how to process what had happened. Feelings of having done something terribly wrong overwhelmed me. I didn't tell anyone. Confused and feeling alone, I continued to see him.

Over the next 24 months, my life spiraled out of control.

My sister, who is eleven months younger than me, became the manager of our high school basketball team. It was my responsibility to drive her to and from basketball practice. One afternoon, as we pulled into a Quick Mart to get gas on the way home, my life took a very dark turn.

The gas station was a place where Hispanic men would gather in the parking lot in hopes of being hired to do odd jobs in the suburbs. When I got out of the car to pump gas, the men, most of them in their twenties and thirties, gathered around the car and began making comments. I got back in my car after pumping the gas. The guys continued to stand around the car. They were not going to let us leave. I talked with several of them and determined which one of them was the leader. He asked for my phone number. Thinking this would placate him, we exchanged phone numbers. They let us go, and we left.

Being from Honduras and adopted into a white family, I had often wondered what it would be like to know other people of Hispanic background. What would it be like to know people of my own kind? Many of you reading these words may not understand. For many who are adopted, while they love their adoptive parents and family at a deep level, there are still lingering questions as you grow up—particularly in adolescence.

Who are my biological parents?
What are they like?
Why did they give me up?
What are people who are of my own ethnicity like?

All of these questions, and many more, relate to the formation of identity. And I, like most adopted children, wrestled with these questions.

So, as a 17-year-old high school student, I texted the man from the gas station. We texted for many weeks until one evening, he sent me the following message, "Come see me at this address." When you are young, you don't have the lens that experience gives you with age. Texting with him for many weeks led me to perceive him to be a trustworthy person.

When I arrived at the address and entered the house, he sexually assaulted me.

I felt scared and lost. As a 17-year-old girl, I didn't fully understand what had happened nor what was happening. Shame and fear began to control me. My grades began to slip. While I was normally a very compliant person, I started lashing out in anger at some of my teachers. I kept going, but without realizing it, something inside of me was dying.

Oddly, I found myself feeling very connected to my attacker. In addition to excelling in academics, I had also excelled in athletics. Now, I was choosing to skip practices in order to be with him. I would tell him "No!" but he would pressure me.

One day I was riding with him in his car and his cell phone rang. I saw a picture of a woman and a little girl light up on his phone. When I asked him about the picture, I found out he was married and had a young daughter.

As a 17-year-old, I went back and told him I don't want to be dating a married man with a daughter. As I talked with him, a small crowd began to gather around us. I could feel anger raging in my heart. In an outburst of emotion, I threw my McDonald's cup at him as hard as I could. He lashed out at me in front of everyone with the words, "She will do anything for money!"

Feeling powerless, I left with one of the other guys in an attempt to make him jealous.

I felt rejected and alone. It was not too long after this episode that the other man also began to manipulate my emotions and my actions. "Go and see this guy," he would say. He started sending me addresses or setting me up with different men from the gas station.

I felt helpless. I began to believe I had no control over my life. I no longer cared about school or much of anything. I started acting out and would get in fights with other students. None of my interactions with men were normal interactions for my age.

I entered my senior year of high school and turned 18. One evening, while attending a basketball game with friends, I accidentally left my cell phone in my car and walked out to the parking lot to get it. A male student approached me and made an inappropriate comment. He sexually assaulted me and filmed the incident on his phone. The next day he shared the video with my classmates at school. He shared that our encounter was consensual when it was not. I was humiliated, hurt, and deeply wounded.

I reported the incident and the police were called. The police officer asked me a lot of questions. But the more questions he asked, the more I knew he was doubting my story. He did not believe me. School administrators questioned my story. The entire incident whittled away at what little life I felt in my soul. I felt isolated and alone.

I graduated from high school and enrolled in a local college. That sounds odd to many people. A young lady being trafficked, yet bettering herself by enrolling in college. I was hurting and confused about so many things. I believed I had gone too far, and there was no way out.

There were times when my trafficker and his people would not let me go to class. There were random times when they would not let me leave. They would make threats and wave their guns. And, there were times when they beat me.

It was in February of my freshman year of college that my parents began to find out about their daughter's secret life. My Mom discovered some of my clothes. "Where did you get the money for these clothes?" she would ask with a tone of desperation.

I was afraid to engage her in giving an explanation, so I avoided telling her the truth. It was also around this time that one of the guys who was close to my trafficker looked at me and said, "We know where you live." I thought to myself, "Wow, they know where my parents live."

I loved my family. I never stopped loving my family. I wanted to do everything I could to protect them. So, in an effort to protect them, I sought shelter at an apartment of one of my Johns[1]. He was one of the calmer ones. In order to hide, I left my cell phone at my parent's home so I could not be tracked. When I settled in at my John's apartment, I went to sleep.

My John had five additional residents. I was a 19-year-old young woman in an apartment with six grown men. Unbeknownst to me at the time, my mom posted the following on her Facebook page the next morning, "We woke up with Martha gone."

I loved my family, but I felt that if they knew what was going on they would disown me. I was so embarrassed. I was so overwhelmed.

---

[1] A "John" is a person who pays for sexual acts.

It was not long until I looked out the window of the apartment one night and was shocked to see an entire row of police cars lining the middle of the parking lot. As I opened the second-floor apartment door to investigate, I made eye contact with one of the police officers.

He scurried up the steps and stood at the threshold of my open door. Looking me straight in the eye he pleaded, "Please go home. Your parents want you to come home." I stood and stared a hole right through him - emotionless. I replied, "I can't go back home."

I had no idea I was the reason all the police were at the apartment. Gripped by fear and shame, I felt paralyzed. I stopped talking with my parents.

One of my friends, who knew some of what was going on in my life, reached out to my mom. She told my mom about my trafficker. His name was Victor. Somehow, my mom was able to make contact with Victor's wife. She apologized to my mom for all that was going on, but Victor's wife didn't know everything. My mom put two and two together and reached out to me.

When my mom reached out to me, we met at a local restaurant. As we talked, she gave me a packet of information. It included information about The WellHouse. I was closed off to her offer of help. It's strange how confused a person can become. So while I actually had grown to hate Victor, I was also trying to protect him.

Within a few months, I found out I was pregnant and let my family back into my life. It didn't go well. Within a few weeks, family members began commenting, "It's like walking on eggshells around you." There was a lot of conflict deep within me and it was outwardly palpable. I felt it, and they felt it, too.

In a few more months, my baby girl was born. While caring for her, I lived in an apartment near Atlanta, but I still stayed with my parents sometimes because I needed their help.

I struggled as a parent. And as I struggled, my parents contacted the Department of Human Resources. I hated my parents for it. My parents won custody. I could only see my baby on supervised visitations. In the midst of all this, I was still seeing Victor, and I was still under his influence as my trafficker.

As a new mother, I needed additional income. I found a job in construction. While working, and through a strange turn of events combined with my own confusion, I was under the impression my boss at my construction job was working with Victor. He messaged me on Facebook to come to his home. When I arrived he said, "I want you to come to a motorcycle event in Florida. You're the entertainment." Another person in my boss' relational network owned a roofing company in Atlanta and wanted me to give myself to some other men so he could get new jobs and contracts. Now there are multiple "Victors" in my life and I became pregnant with my second child.

There were several guys living in the apartment where I was now residing. The guys in the house continued to get physical. I got into an argument with one of them and he beat me. One of the men was sleeping on the couch and woke up and asked the man, "Did you just beat her?" When he said "Yes," the man rolled over and went back to sleep. I tried to cope with it all by locking myself in the bathroom. Oddly, I had grown numb to it all and willingly accepted the abuse.

While I was not speaking to my family at this time, I was growing determined to get my daughter out of it. I wanted it all to be over. I faced repeated beatings. When I was six months pregnant, Victor began to leave me alone. I wanted out of my circumstance, but I couldn't figure out how to get out.

I woke up one morning and began to clean the apartment. As soon as I sat my daughter down I heard a knock at the door. When I opened the door, two police officers greeted me. They informed me there were 13 warrants issued for my arrest.

The police officers dropped me at the jail. I sat, all alone, in a holding cell. Then the Police officers spent two hours talking with me. Because I had felt betrayed by the police before, I chose to shut down and not talk.

One of the police officers interrupted the interrogation and asked, "You want to process her or can I talk with her?" I would later grow to understand how he was going far beyond his job and seeking to be helpful. When he began asking me questions, I chose to be difficult. But, over and over, he would pause and ask me with sincerity, "Are you okay?"

As he tried to get me to open up and talk about my story, I didn't trust him. I was very resistant to talk with him or anyone. But I did notice that he seemed different. He seemed to genuinely care. Over the course of many hours, I began to open up more and more. I noticed that he listened. He really listened, and I could tell he believed me. He really believed me.

He personally bought me lunch and supper as we talked throughout the afternoon. He later confided that "Your mom told me what's going on." When I realized he knew my family, my heart began to open up and I told him everything. I told him about Victor. I gave other names, addresses, and phone numbers.

The police officer began pleading with me to go to The WellHouse. This turned into a yelling and shouting match. He kept saying, "You need help! Your daughter needs her mom, and the only way for her to have her mom is for her mom to get the help she needs!"

The officer notified my parents regarding my whereabouts. I was so ashamed. I wouldn't talk with them, but I would soon learn that my mom never stopped trying to reach out to me. I put them through the worst of everything. They had to watch their little girl be torn into pieces.

As we journeyed into the afternoon and evening, the police officer began encouraging me to talk with my mom and then go to The WellHouse. What I didn't know at the time was that my mom had figured out what was going on in my life. She and my dad had already been in conversation with the police about their belief that I was being trafficked and their hopes for their daughter to connect with the people of The WellHouse.

I went to The WellHouse with a bad attitude. I also told myself I would do three months and then go home. I had a huge chip on my shoulder, and I didn't want to be friends with anyone, whether it was with the staff or other residents. I wouldn't even shake anyone's hand.

The journey at The WellHouse was difficult but worth it. The WellHouse was a place where I experienced restoration. Again, it was not all easy, but I am thankful I chose to go and persevere through its ministry. I experienced love there. I experienced the structure I needed to help me see myself as a person of worth and dignity. I made dear friends at The WellHouse. I learned to share my problems rather than taking off and running. My faith in males was restored through a combination of spiritual development and programs and structure at The WellHouse. I am thankful for the new life that I now have.

Before I went to The WellHouse, I was broken and angry and questioning God. Now, my faith in God has been restored and I am thankful for my relationship with Him. I am still in shock at how good my life is right now. I never thought I could be happy again. I didn't think I'd make it past 21, but I am living a happy and productive life. I am working and I am back in school. I am thankful I stuck it out. I know I was a hard case.

If you are wondering if human trafficking can happen around you, even among upper-middle-class teenagers, I hope my story helps awaken you. Trafficking happens to people of all backgrounds, including those who grow up in a nice family living in an upscale neighborhood.

As a teenage girl, I felt invincible. I never thought I would lose control and end up in a life that I would never choose. None of us are invincible, no matter how much love we have or the type of family we come from.

Today, I am working a full-time job that I greatly enjoy. My relationships with my mom and dad, and my entire family, are restored. I am working through having full custody of my two daughters, and I am looking forward to the future with a new sense of hope.

And I feel at home. ✧

A PART OF OUR PROCESS

*F*ROM VICTIM TO SURVIVOR.
   Within a short time, the recovering victim transitions to survivor as she leaves behind the horrific victimization she has endured.

The Rescue Supervisor arranges safe passage for the survivor and ensures her journey is not traumatic. She travels with assistance by bus, train, plane, or car to The WellHouse campus in Alabama.

We partner with organizations such as Trafficking Hope and Falcon Ministries who assist with travel and pick-up.

The Rescue Supervisor maintains contact along the way and is ready to intervene if necessary.

It is always a relief to hear the words:

"She is safe."

LUCIE

Come, everyone who thirsts,
   come to the waters;
and he who has no money,
   come, buy and eat!
Come, buy wine and milk
   without money and without price.
Why do you spend your money for that which is not bread,
   and your labor for that which does not satisfy?
Listen diligently to me, and eat what is good,
   and delight yourselves in rich food.
Incline your ear, and come to me;
   hear, that your soul may live;

–Isaiah 55

Whenever I'm hungry, I eat. Such a simple thing. That's how it's supposed to be. It's not something that I take for granted.

My parents tried. At first they tried together, but that didn't work out so well. The façade of a happy middle class family that they had been striving for broke down when they divorced. I was 5. My mother and I moved from a 3 bedroom brick home into a dilapidated trailer on the other side of my grandparent's house.

On weekends and summers, I spent as much time as was allowed with my dad. That was in various dwellings over the years....some that approached the doorway to that middle class life. Some...not so much.

Poverty was a loyal companion. But it's an insidious companion that worms its way into every aspect of one's life. Being poor was the only thing I could depend on to be true.

The majority of my life was spent on a hill in rural southwest Georgia where I grew like the weeds in the woods. I never really felt like I belonged, but I was unaware of the world on the other side of that dirt driveway.

At 15, I met a boy at church. Although we were friends, we became intimate very quickly. I reckon we were both running from something... or maybe to something else. Either way, I got pregnant. Against my family's wishes, I got married one month after my 16th birthday. I did not feel like

I had another option.

I had been the founder and president of my high school's Bible study club. I had wanted to be a preacher, even though my Assembly of God background disapproved. I stepped down from that role out of respect for the position. I had wanted to be an English teacher like my Mama had been before her divorce. Even though I graduated high school, I never even took the ACT or SAT.

I decided that I wanted to coach college football. My love of the game had persisted through the years, because I had grown up playing and watching football with my boy cousins. But one of them became curious about my 12 yr old female body. I didn't tell anyone what happened for a long time afterwards. Just like my 5 year self had been a target for someone else. That, too, was a secret my soul had kept.

Life had taught me a lot more than I needed to know way earlier than it should've. And it seemingly snatched dreams at will. I continued going to school and my child's father graduated and got a job. It wasn't enough, especially after I got pregnant again. He joined the Army in an attempt to support us better. I moved to another city in southwest Florida and tried to be everything I needed to be.

My mother died 5 weeks after my 2nd son was born. My eldest child was 22 months old. My husband was off in a different state for Army job training.

I was alone

and only 18.

The next several years saw my babies grow into toddlers, then toddlers into young children. We lived in Germany for a few of those years. My husband was always gone...whether in the field training or Iraq- where 2 deployments brought 27 months of fear of a knock on my door by a chaplain. Me and him were friends by choice but I was forced to be his lover whenever he was home. That was my job as a wife and he never failed to remind me of that.

He got out of the Army and we moved back to Florida. It wasn't long before we couldn't maintain our unhealthy and abusive relationship any longer. After moving to South Alabama, we tried to make it work together for a time.

After our divorce, he got married again immediately. He had stability. A home. Support. The title of a veteran in a place where military worship is rampant. I had none of that and my boys ended up living full-time with him. That's also when child support started being taken from my check. It is humanly impossible to outwork the limitations that half of a minimum wage paycheck brings.

I met someone else and attached myself to yet another dream of someone wanting me. He capitalized on my vulnerability, and our baby arrived about a year later.

There was never enough of anything. Money. Food. Transportation. Shelter.

Respect. We were in and out of homeless shelters and pay-by-the-hour type of motels. He was in and out of relationships with other women.

Rich people don't go to jail. They may go to prison if they do something terribly bad. But jail is for poor folks. During the transition between my prior life and the one that I was then living, I had gotten pulled over by a traffic cop. My ex-husband hadn't given me the insurance card and I couldn't prove that I wasn't driving illegally. They levied a $220 ticket on me for not having proof.

That's not a lot of money. But survival is expensive and that ticket had long past turned into a warrant by the time my youngest son was walking.

The relationship with my third child's father progressed to the point of physical abuse. We were both trapped, with the only difference being I didn't have a way out. After one particularly intense fight, he called the police on me then left the premises. They arrested me for that warrant.

3 weeks in county jail didn't count against any fine. That's just how long it took to wait for the once-a-month judge to show up. I got out with the threat of that bill still over my head.

There was no going home. I didn't have one left. He had taken our 1 year old and moved in with his other girlfriend. Everything of mine had already been picked up off the side of the road like the rest of the garbage.

I had no ID. No birth certificate. No social security card. And 30 days to pay my fine or go back to jail.

I was hungry. But that wasn't new. I'd been hungry my entire life.

I walked up to the church that I'd been attending and volunteering at. It's sole purpose was outreach ministry, targeting the have-nots. I knew what days were hot food days and which days were bread days and which days I could shower and do laundry. I happened to stop by on a bread day. I was a familiar face there.

Unfortunately, the pastor had a sickness that I wasn't aware of at the time. He saw the opportunity to manipulate someone who had nothing. He knew my options for survival were few and far between.

He told me to ride with him so that we could talk. He knew my situation and said he could help. We traveled to the outskirts of town, where the tall pine trees wouldn't tell any secrets. He unzipped his pants then pulled his pistol out and sat it down. He explained that he could help me. He spoke with the same charisma that he did from the pulpit, but there was a seriousness about his tone that made me understand. He reminded me that I was a throw-away. That no one would miss me. That I was estranged from my family and had no friends left. That no one would ever find me.

Now I'm not scared of much, and I wasn't scared of him.

But I'm also not stupid. And that man meant what he said. I only had one viable option.

He "adopted" me. He put me into an apartment with another woman that had long been under his control. He introduced me to his main mistress. He set me up with his friends. They did help me get some of my identifying documents, but I had to earn every bit of it.

I was just trying to survive.

Time passed, with him sinking his claws deeper into every facet of my life. He kicked the other woman out on the street on Christmas Eve because she wouldn't cooperate fully. It all got old so quickly.

I spoke up. At first to a good friend, then to the associate pastor and his wife. They helped arrange a meeting with the regional directors of the denomination, and I explained what had been happening. I just wanted him to stop hurting people.

But I hadn't been the first. And wouldn't be the last.

The denomination let him resign on his own terms with his own story. Rumors abound though, and I became shunned by even the most ostracized of society's members. I lost my shelter and my job because his monstrous octopus tentacles of influence reached far and wide.

I got a job working overnight at a gas station. I slept where I could. Some nights it was in alleys behind downtown buildings. Some nights it was abandoned houses. Some nights it was on the couch of someone who barely had enough of their own to share. I worked. But my minimum wage paycheck cut in half by child support didn't allow for any hindrances. And I still had plenty of those.

Eventually, I made enough to rent my own place. A couple hundred dollars a month is sufficient for a home with no electricity, no hot water, and bullet holes in the front door.

I would get messages from random numbers threatening me as I walked miles back and forth to my jobs. The pastor even served me a notice that they were suing me if I didn't recant everything.

Sue me for what?? I still owed fines and was dodging yet another warrant for non-payment. I had nothing to my name.

As I look back, I realize that I wasn't being just told to cease and desist. The point was to absolutely destroy me.

Well, no one ever taught me how to give up so I simply didn't know how. I walked miles every day to my job and worked every hour that was available to me. I just kept trying.

But it was never enough. Not enough time. Not enough money. Not enough air to breathe in a town where one can suffocate without support.

I hopped on a greyhound bus and landed in northeast Ohio. It was a different planet with tall buildings and hundreds of thousands of people. Most importantly, there was public transportation. Within 48 hours, I found a job working at a factory for a temp service. I slept on the living room floor between the couch and wall of a friend of a friend. I was able to get another job and enroll in college. Unfortunately, the human body can only do so much. After several weeks of not sleeping for 4-5 days at a time, I couldn't stay in school. Once again, I couldn't outwork the limitations that had been placed on me, no matter how much I tried.

I was able to get a vehicle, though, a beat up old Ranger that had seen better days. It became my lifeline. People have no idea what being stranded is until they've had their legs as the only mode of transportation for years.

I headed back down to south Alabama. Even with wheels though, if nothing changes then nothing changes. Once again, I got caught up in an abusive relationship, because I needed a roof over my head. Survival is rarely pretty, but it's especially treacherous for a woman. There were times that my body paid the price for the room under his supervision. Even with a job, I could never get out of that role.

My tolerance for abuse and manipulation and forced prostitution had gotten pretty thin by that point. After only a couple of months, I moved back to Ohio.

It was so cold and my only shelter was my pickup truck. I couldn't afford gas to idle it for the heat, but I managed for a short time. I was so tired from a life like that makes a person turn old before their time.

On a lark, I decided to go back down to Alabama and try it again there.

On the way down, the wheel bearings of my truck locked up and I slept in it for the last time at a Marathon station about halfway between Louisville and Cincinnati. I had not a single dollar to my name. Nowhere to go and no way to get there.

But I had to do *something.*

The next morning, I hitched a ride from there to a truck stop. I only wanted a ride south. But once again, I was hungry. And once again, I had to barter my body in order to survive. A few hours after that, another driver allowed me to ride with him. He brought me down to Birmingham. He was respectful

My resolve grew roots as I spent the night at the truck stop in an off-to-the-side booth. I decided that I would never again give what I don't want to give simply to survive. I would not.

I reached out to the only person I knew in the area. She had associations with The WellHouse and facilitated the communications necessary for me to go there.

I didn't really want to go. I didn't even want to stay when I got there. I didn't trust anyone or anything. I didn't believe that anything could be free, especially room and board and care. I didn't want to live in a home with other women and I didn't want to attend meetings about drugs that I'd never taken.

Regardless of what I wanted, though, what I needed was a place to land and satisfy my exhausting hunger. So I did, reluctantly, at The WellHouse.

The people that worked there earned my hesitant trust. They believed in me and helped me face myself.

I had known about the strength of God. About His power. About His mercy. About His love. I had experienced all of those things. I could sing about Jesus being my friend with full honesty.

But I had never known the peace of God. The rest that comes in stillness that's safe. It found me there 5 years ago.

I'm still not where I want to be in life. My goals and dreams have evolved with my progression. It wasn't a light-bulb switch that all of a sudden made life grand. I still struggle sometimes.

But I do not have to trade sexual favors for survival. I haven't had to in a long time.

I have a career where I can take care of myself without having to depend on someone who might take advantage of me. I've been able to reconnect with my children and family. A little support can go a long way. I'll forever be grateful for that.

Because now I can eat when I'm hungry.

And that's satisfying to my soul. ❖

A PART OF OUR PROCESS

*T*O THE WELLHOUSE TRAUMA CENTER. For the first time, she is safe.

She arrives with few belongings.

The pain on her face begins to subside as she slowly exhales a lifetime of trauma.

A clean room and bed, a nice shower, and a home-cooked meal all spell safety and hope.

During her time in the Trauma Center, usually two weeks, the survivor is nurtured and met with a sense of safety. She is able to begin building trust. She meets her Home Coordinator, who cares for her as she settles in, and her Trauma Therapist, who shows empathy and compassion as they perform assessments in order to measure current needs and develop a treatment plan customized to those needs. That plan will follow her as she moves from the Trauma Center to the first phase of the program. The plan is adjusted as she meets goals.

She is beginning to heal.

JANE

For you formed my inward parts;
   you knitted me together in my mother's womb.
I praise you, for I am fearfully and wonderfully made.
Wonderful are your works;
   my soul knows it very well.

Psalm 139:7–16

I always thought it was the Devil who had been chasing me.

My mom had me when she was 15 years old. When she found out she was pregnant, she ran away from Louisiana to Alabama, to go to a program for unwed teen mothers in Birmingham. I was born there and then my mom's dad came to bring us back home to Crowville, Louisiana.

I hadn't known my biological dad, Buster, as a child but he came around a few times while growing up. Eventually, my mom met another man. They married and had two more kids. When I was little, I was curious about other kids sexually, and had to go to the hospital all the time because I would hold my bladder and bowels. I wouldn't go to the bathroom. And I was also a bed-wetter. All of these are signs of sexual abuse, and although I don't have vivid memories of it, I believe I was molested by someone when I was really young.

Crowville is a very rural place and I grew up on a farm. I never wanted to be out there with my mom, because she was an addict and alcoholic and would either be passed out asleep or having teenage guys coming over. These are my first real memories at about 6 or 7 years old. My adoptive dad was a hard worker and a great provider. They had a girl together, my sister, and I loved her. My adoptive dad kept us in church and sports growing up, but I just never felt like I belonged.

The most stable and happy thing for me to do was go to my grandparent's house, so I spent a lot of my time there. My Grandfather was everything to me. He loved the outdoors and so I did too. He taught me how to fish and hunt, gave me encyclopedias, and took me camping and deep-sea fishing.

However, he wasn't always the good man that I knew. Before I was born, apparently he was a pretty bad alcoholic. He beat my grandmother and she even lost a child that she'd been pregnant with as a result of him getting drunk and beating her up. But the story goes, as soon as he laid eyes on me when I was born, he quit drinking, and became a good man. That made me feel valued and loved, and I loved him back for it. I never knew him to be drunk or violent.

When I was 9, my mom and adoptive father got divorced. My mom took off. My adoptive dad took custody of me, and so I lived with him and his other 2 daughters. I was around his parents and my aunt a good bit of the time. But to them, I was the daughter of the woman that left. They called me a bastard, and it was the first time I learned the word and what it meant. I felt what it meant when my grandma and aunt told my sisters that I wasn't their real sister. I believed that being adopted meant that you were unlovable. This belief started to impact my behavior. I began to withdraw.

At age 12, my Grandfather, who I loved dearly, was diagnosed with polycystic kidney disease. My grandmother took me to a class to learn how to dialyze him, which had to be done at home 3 times a week. She worked a hard job in a factory, and she needed the help. I didn't mind or think twice about caring for my grandfather, because I loved him so much. I took him to show and tell at school to show the other kids how the kidney worked. Around this time, my mom had come back into the picture, so I saw her some too.

When I was 14, my 27-year-old aunt tragically fell down seven flights of stairs at work. The fall left her paralyzed and a quadriplegic. Even though my aunt got a multi-million dollar settlement from her accident, she needed someone to take care of her. So, my grandmother made me quit school. I handed in my textbooks so that I could help take care of my grandfather and my aunt. He needed his dialysis three times a week and she needed around-the-clock care.

Life was too much to bear as a young teenager. I took all of my aunt's medication and attempted suicide...

but, I didn't die.

At 15, I met Robby. After we started dating, I moved in with him and his parents in another town. He smoked crack cocaine and got me hooked on it too. It was my first experience with drugs. When he was high, he was violent and abusive. He would beat me up, even breaking my ribs. I stayed with him for years. Later, Robby and I started doing crystal meth. He became dependent on the needle and continued to be violent. I have damage to my right eye today from one of his hard-thrown punches. I didn't want to stay, but I also didn't know what else to do. Plus, I liked being high.

Every now and then, I'd see my mom and she could see what he'd been doing to me. She would freak out about it, but that didn't change anything. He made me feel worthless, but I would keep going back. I've learned now that this was deep-rooted trauma bonding.

He kept trying to beat the spirit out of me and sometimes he would win. But after my grandmother and my grandfather died, my life changed forever. It ripped a hole in my heart and I really didn't care about life much after losing them. Finally, Robby and I split up, and I quit drugs. But at 21, I was pregnant with my first child. When I was 9 months pregnant, Robby snatched me up and put a gun to my head, but somehow, I got away. I had my daughter and named her Megan.

About a year later, I met a man named Chris and we fell in love and got married. I enrolled in a junior college for nursing school. The first week of class, I found out we were pregnant with my second child, our son Parker. We loved our children very much. Things had started to look better, but not for too long.

Chris drank heavily. I would drink too, and eventually we started doing cocaine. Chris was a great person and not abusive, which was a plus. But after everything in my life, I was beyond hurt. I had a lot of anger and rage, and I would take it out on Chris. We had our third child, Alex, but by this time we were struggling in our marriage and substance abuse. Chris was drunk so often that it was hard for him to work and keep down a job.

One night, I went to a bad area of town in Alexandria to get us drugs. I pulled up at a stop sign and was texting the dealer. The next thing I knew, 2 Crips[2] came to the window, held me at gunpoint, and they made me drive to an abandoned house where they raped me. I begged them to use a condom.

WHAM!

They pistol-whipped me. They put me in the back seat, all bloody and beaten, and as I was going in and out of consciousness I heard them say they were going to finish me off. Instead, they backed my car up and off into a ditch and got it stuck, and they ran off. A couple came and found me and called an ambulance.

When I got released from the hospital and went home, I told Chris what happened, and he said he would never touch me again. I was soiled goods after what the Crips did to me. He took emergency custody of my kids and took off with them.

So, I was left alone in the house.

It was all way too much. Through my tears, I saw a plate of cocaine and crack, and I did it all night. I felt like the devil was right there with me. And then I heard a knock on the door.

[2] Members of a specific gang called the Crips

Looking through the blankets nailed on my window, I could see it was Buster, my biological dad.

Buster always had a way of showing up when things were wrong. He was a crack addict, a junkie, a drunk, and a mean person. I let him in, gave him the rest of my drugs, and said I was going to lie down. I had been up for two days on cocaine and crack and then I took 4 Xanax bars so I was ready to pass out.

I woke up in the dark to someone having sex with me. When my vision cleared, I could see that it was Buster. I started screaming "Get up! Get up!" and pushing him off. He was like, "What? What? I'm not doing anything wrong." I couldn't even cry or yell... I was in shock. As he was leaving, he turned around and said, "You know what, it was as good as I always thought it would be."

After that, I knew I had to stop the drugs. I finally really wanted to. I went to a treatment center in Franklinton. I was able to do some healing and was really trying to live sober, which I did for a while. But I relapsed after 18 months.

I made my way back to Alexandria, and checked in at a motel called Poplar Motor Lodge. I started selling drugs to pay for my room and would have sex with guys in exchange for them paying for the room. This new home with pink cinder block walls felt cold, even though for the first time in my life I wasn't taking care of someone else. I experienced a taste of freedom. Maybe it was selfish, but to just be on my own for a minute, make my own decisions, be high, and focus on me, it felt good.

There was an 18-year-old named Javier who tattooed and lived next door at Poplar. We became friends, and I learned he was in the Cartel. Javier was trading tattoos for drugs. I would walk out to the drink machine, and some of his clients would come talk to me and want to hook up. I was hustling off of Javier's hustle. He knew I was by myself. One day he asked me to go to New Orleans. We walked into a hotel room there, and I met Santiago, who would become my first pimp.

Santiago asked me to show him my boobs. I was strung out on meth, so I did. He began taking photos. Then Javier sold me to Santiago for a bottle of Lortabs.

I remember thinking "I'm not up for grabs... I'm a person". At the same time, I didn't think I had already been prostituting at Poplar. In my mind, I was just surviving. Javier knew that if he got me away from Poplar, it was going to be hard for me to get away.

I soon saw my photo as an ad on a trafficking website. My first working name was Lacey Lollipop.

So, I would have sex and Santiago got the money. He said to me, "This is what you're gonna do, make some money, honey." I asked him what would happen if the Johns weren't nice. Santiago said "Bitch, you better see them as green 'cause they are money." He was dominating and violent, and he hit me with clothes hangers.

One of my Johns gave me a rainbow knife. Santiago and I got into a fight, and he was hitting me. He didn't quit, and I ran into the bathroom and slammed the door. I was on the floor, holding the door shut with my feet, when he came over the door at me. I chopped his thumb off with the rainbow knife. His thumb was barely attached as we approached the front desk.

The police came, and they ended up taking me to the psych ward in Baton Rouge. This is how I got away from Santiago, and I left the psych ward walking away with nothing. But I had seen Santiago post on the trafficking website. I knew how to post an ad and make some money. So I posted my own ads.

I was in contact with a friend from Nashville who knew what I was doing, and her advice led me into a new world: a new level of pimps and feds and the prison system. I needed someone to help take care of me. I was introduced to Flaco, my next pimp.

Flaco named me Cherry. He came from money and had plenty of money. He drove nice cars and could drop me like a snap. He had dope boy money, from the feds, a recording studio, and an apartment complex. Flaco was married, and he had things in his wife's name that the cops couldn't seize. He gave me a room in the apartment complex. He got me off meth. My quota[3] was $500 / day and he would let me go to bed at midnight. He stocked me up with healthy foods and vitamins, saying that he wanted me to take care of myself. I thought he hung the moon.

Flaco was a preacher. Preacher by day and criminal by night. After I worked I'd get in the car and give him my money like he said to. He didn't like women to talk unless they were talked to first. If I needed my laundry done, his wife would wash my laundry, and he would reward me with expensive gifts.

I never liked this life, but when shame sets in far enough, going home doesn't seem like an option. I missed my kids desperately but they were so far away.

My kids are better off without me.

Every day I woke up, I had a death wish. I would curse God and say "what you got for me today?!". I would set out to do the most dangerous and dumb things on purpose, to see if could die. I didn't care.

I left Flaco a couple times. Eventually, he put me up in a bad part of town, put $1,000 loafers on me and a diamond tennis bracelet setting me up to get robbed. Maybe he was

---

3 Quota: A set amount of money that a trafficking victim must make each night. If the victim returns without meeting the quota, she is typically beaten and sent back out on the street to earn the rest. (from Shared Hope International at https://sharedhope.org)

done with me. He was a real pimp, not a gorilla[4] pimp but a business pimp. I would stay with him for a while, then leave again. Once I went to live with one of my johns.

He was someone who respected my hustle but said he cared about me. We had somewhat of a normal life living together... I would go get a room for the day, get my money, and go lay down with him that night. But to me it was totally business, I was so in the life and was able to go escort for a couple hours, then come home and cook and watch movies. We had cats and a yard and I planted flowers. This dude was a life changer for me.

One weekend when I came back, his car was in the carport but the door was locked and he wasn't answering it. He wouldn't answer the phone either. I kicked the door in. In the house with him there was another woman, and I couldn't even make a sound. It was like hot helium, just pain seeping out. He was surprised at the fact that I really maybe loved him. He pretended like he had no idea who I was. This new girl had just come out of federal prison and someone had sold her to him.

After that, I got into one bad situation after another with drugs and the Bloods[5]. I had gotten hurt and didn't care. One time, I started talking to these crazy people about Jesus, but I got away from them and started walking down the street in Nashville with $6 in my pocket. I usually hadn't been doing drugs around people, no crack or cocaine, only meth during escorting because it keeps you up all night.

I made my way back to Alexandria, Louisiana and got a hotel room and tried to regroup. I got on a dating website, and that's where I met Cedric. We would talk on the phone for hours, and we really connected. He drove from Alabama

---

[4] Gorilla pimp: a pimp who controls his victims almost entirely through physical violence and force. (from Shared Hope International at https://sharedhope.org)

[5] Bloods: the name of a specific gang.

to Louisiana to pick me up and we went back to Alabama and got a hotel room. Instantly we just fell in love and it went from there. I was still prostituting and eventually I told him about it, and he said it was okay. He said that he and another girl had done a trafficking website in South Carolina and then she got pregnant. Cedric tried to get me to come move in with his family, but I said no. I was addicted to meth, and he was not.

After Cedric got on drugs with me, it went downhill from there. He became abusive. Three times he put me in a neck brace from choking me unconscious, he broke my arm, and knocked out my front tooth. I found out that he was sending his baby momma money off my body. He was prostituting me to take care of her, and maybe that was his plan all along. He abused me and I made the money for him. And he did what he wanted with the money, including sending it back to this girl in North Carolina. It's like he was pretending all along... all the signs are there.

I got raped and robbed at gunpoint several times while I was with him. He never had any sympathy and always blamed me. We went all over the Southeast. In 2017. I was arrested in a prostitution sting. Trafficking Hope came in and tried to get me to go to The WellHouse. I lied to them and chose to go to jail. Cedric bonded me out the next day on prostitution.

The next couple of years were a complete nightmare. He made me work all through the night. We stayed together another 2 years, drugging, traveling, escorting, and him abusing me. We went back to Alabama and he met someone else. He left me tied up in a hotel. Somehow I got loose and there was a trucker parked at the Hardee's across from the hotel. I knocked and said, "Where you going?" He said, "Orlando, FL." So I went too. I always went to wherever casinos were, thinking maybe God would give me a miracle at a table and

I'd win big to get out of the life.

Instead, that's when I remembered and called The Well-House. Dixie answered the phone and did an assessment with me, and she called back the next day to say I was going there. I was so sick, and I didn't have any drugs. They all had heroin and I didn't want that. I left my high heels and a bag of weed and wrote to the housekeepers a note that said "enjoy." I had on a truck stop moo-moo dress and nothing else. I rode on a bus all the way from Orlando to Birmingham with a couple changeovers. At one changeover in Montgomery, the devil was waiting.

Cedric was there. When we arrived at the station, the bus drivers got into a big argument and our driver said she would not be driving us to Birmingham. The longer we sat there I thought, "I should just ask Cedric to come and get me." Instead I asked God to give me some strength. A random driver got in the seat and began to take us to Birmingham.

When I first got to The WellHouse in 2019, I was in the Trauma Center for three days. The next step was TIS (The Immediate Shelter). You can be in that house for about 3-4 months but I was there six weeks before we decided that I was moving along fast with my recovery. We decided to go ahead and move me up to the next house- NSF (Next Steps to Freedom). Here is where my recovery really began.

I was used to having a mask on so everyone would see what I wanted them to see and I would never stay around people very long so they couldn't see how messed up I was, so it was no surprise when staff thought I was doing well. It was not long at NSF before my anger issues and my emotional outbursts came to the surface. Then, they decided to move me back down to TIS. I had already enrolled at the local community college, but I had to drop out when I moved back down to the first house. They decided that I needed more therapy, which I did, so I was down there for about 2 months. I made some good progress and actually tried to work through the problems that I had instead of masking them.

At first I was angry about having to go back, and thought about leaving, but then a calmness came over me and I accepted it. When I surrendered to God in that moment and went back down to TIS I think that's when everything changed. Eventually I did then move back to NSF, and I enrolled back into school at another school for online classes. I actually graduated from the program in 2020. I was able to get a full-time job in October of 2020 as a seamstress and moved up into the apartments in 2021.

When I first arrived, I was completely broken and I felt dead inside. Since I've been here I've become closer to Jesus Christ and I've been restored to my whole family. I feel like I've been healed from all the pain that I've been through in life and I've learned how to control my emotions better. I am a junior at Southern New Hampshire University majoring in Criminal Justice and I have a full-time job as an industrial seamstress. I took an anti-human trafficking course so I can volunteer with Trafficking Hope. My goal is to work with law enforcement to help transport women. I never thought that my life would be this productive. I never saw past the life that I was living in and I never thought it was possible to come out of it, but with the help of the staff at The Well-House and all of the volunteers and the people who have poured so much love into me, I now love myself and I have a bright future. I have changed so much from the bitter, broken, and damaged woman that I was. I am loved and I have love to give. I want to work in the corrections field because a lot of traffickers target women who are in prison and who need help. I feel like God is really putting it on my heart to use my degree to work in the prison system. I just can't wait to see what the rest of this journey looks like. I love The Well-House and they will always be a part of my life.

Now, I can say that I have a lot of joy in my heart. That is what is a miracle to me, that I have so much joy and love to give. And it is only from God.

I thought it was the Devil who wouldn't leave me alone, but God was with me the whole time. I know that deep down in my bones. God is with me. ✧

A PART OF OUR PROCESS

*T*RAUMA & GRIEF COUNSELING. The WellHouse has two licensed therapists on staff who are skilled in trauma therapy and utilize therapeutic modalities that best address complex trauma experienced by a survivor of human trafficking.

In the beginning, the survivor meets several times a week with her therapist for supportive counseling to begin addressing her trauma.

The therapist follows her as she transitions into the Immediate Shelter (TIS), and has a treatment plan ready for the two of them to begin. This plan is also shared with other pertinent staff so the entire team can assist with her healing process.

She is getting support.

"Addressing trauma involves assessing a survivor's ability to feel emotions. Building internal stability is essential. The building process includes active listening, which is paramount to creating a sense of safety for a survivor. Often, in session, a survivor will say she has never been heard before. From the moment a survivor walks into the therapy room, the therapist is observing.

- Does that survivor knock on the door or does she just walk in?
- Is the survivor able to have eye contact with the therapist?

Everything about a survivor, both verbal and nonverbal, is communicating something. As the sessions continue, the internal stability increases. She will begin by sharing a part of her trauma narrative from a 50,000 feet level. It will sound as if she is reporting the weather. Affect will be nonexistent and the therapist will know that she is very disconnected from her story. In time, as her internal sense of safety continues to build, she will retell her story with more affect. She is becoming alive and feeling!"

- Corinne, staff member

GRACE

For by grace you have been saved through faith. And this is not your own doing; it is the gift of God, not a result of works, so that no one may boast. For we are his workmanship, created in Christ Jesus for good works, which God prepared beforehand, that we should walk in them.

Ephesians 2:1–10

You can call me Grace.

I don't remember all that much about my life before I was adopted. I know that Child Protective Services took my brother and me away from my biological mom several times. We went back and forth from her house to foster care over and over again. At both places, really bad things happened.

My mother always had a lot of men in and out of her place. They were not good people and I'm sure this is why we were taken to foster care. But bad things happened in foster care too. I was sexually abused by several people in both of these places and the fragmented memories haunt me. I was finally adopted at the age of five, right before I started Kindergarten.

My adoptive Dad and Mom were in school for social work. They came to our town on a mission trip and met my biological mom at one of their community programs. They loved us so much they decided to stay in our town and build a ministry. When they finally adopted my brother and me, they brought us to an awesome church. There were lots of kids and people from all kinds of backgrounds. I loved it. I remember making up my mind that I was going to become a normal little girl, just like the people at my new school and church. It was strange, though. The harder I tried to be normal, the more impossible it felt.

I had a terrible pit of sadness inside my heart. I was fearful and worried. I couldn't stop wetting the bed. The thing I couldn't tell my new parents was horribly shameful. The truth was that some of the boys who participated in their home ministry were now molesting me. Why did this keep happening? I tried to be a good kid but everyone knew I was troubled. I didn't understand healthy boundaries, and I never felt safe.

But even with all of that, my parents continued to love me. When I was in middle school, I was referred to an after school program that helped kids with problems like mine. I was very nervous to go but, to my surprise, I loved it! The people in that program had a way of showing love that felt different and pure and beautiful. They had a counselor that helped me talk about things. The program staff met with my school and explained my background and current challenges. After that, my teachers took extra time to support and encourage me. For the first time in my life, I felt strong.

I graduated from high school with a proud family and lots of hope for my future.

Only a few weeks later, I met the man who made me do unspeakable things. I still remember the day we met. I parked my car at the neighborhood grocery store and the security guard walked over to me. "Ma'am", he said, "You parked your car in the wrong spot." With the sassy arrogance of a high school graduate, I snapped, "NO I did not!" His face angered, "Ma'am, you are in a handicapped spot." I paled. Then he smiled and laughed a little. "I'm messing with you. I just wanted to find a way to talk to you." Right there, in the middle of the parking lot, my little, young self, fell in love with the security guard. I was smitten.

Everything about our relationship moved at warp speed. My parents were horrified when I told them I wanted to leave home and move in with him. They argued, cried, begged and eventually threatened to disown me. None of that mattered to me. I was seventeen years old and ready to marry a 32 year old career criminal who promised me love.

The abuse came rapidly, as well. In our home together, he demanded possession of everything I had, including my paychecks, my bank account, and my phone. I worked a lot during that time and he was always worried that I was talking with other men. In his jealousy, he punched me with his fists, hit me with objects, berated me, and forced himself on me repeatedly. At some point, I started thinking about running away.

I found a women's shelter that agreed to secretly provide me with counseling and a place to stay. They were a great help to me until one day when he called. He asked if he could see me and, against all my better judgment, I agreed. When we met, I was surprised to see him with a tricked out car, a fancy watch and an expensive suit and shoes. Who knows how he came into this particular stash of money? He wouldn't tell me. But he was so sweet and charming, I agreed to go back. Besides, by that time, I was pregnant with his baby.

Like everything else, we ran through the money in record time. Before I knew it, we were flat broke. He decided the thing to do was to move to Mississippi and start fresh. We drove west and landed at the first hotel who would hire me to be a desk clerk in exchange for a room. My son was only a baby then and I think they were trying to help us. But my husband was not happy with the arrangement. Because all of my wages went to pay for the room, there was no money for anything else. "I took care of you when you had nothing!" he railed. "Now it's time for you to take care of us." I knew what he meant because he had conditioned me for it for years. After so much abuse, I hardly cared what happened to me.

I noticed men started coming by the hotel after the local construction projects closed. They were just kind of hanging out around the lobby when my shift ended. When my husband looked my way, I knew what I would have to do next. I still remember the first time it happened. I tried to let go of my body and exist somewhere else but I couldn't. My baby was right next to me during the whole thing.

It was a dark and devastating time. I knew that, in order to protect my son, I had to find a way out. One night, while I was alone, I decided to call my brother. Together, we made an escape plan. When my son and I were able to get away, I was elated. But before I knew it, he found us. This time, he grabbed me by my hair and dragged me screaming from my brother's house. He threw the baby and me in the car and kept us there for three days. I had no idea where we were going but eventually, we had to stop for gas. When we pulled up to the pump, he grabbed my hair in his fist again. "Do not move." he growled and jerked my hair so suddenly that my body literally lifted off the seat! Screaming as he crossed in front of the car toward the gas pump, I realized that I had moved from the passenger to the driver's seat. I stepped hard onto the gas pedal, knocked him onto the ground, and left him forever.

Again, I found myself vowing to become a regular, healthy, productive woman.

It was difficult, though. I reached out to my parents for help but it was complicated. During the bad time, they arranged for a legal emancipation from me. They did offer to take care of my baby boy, though. They took my baby and dropped me off at a homeless shelter.

Sometimes, things that look great at first glance turn out terribly wrong.

But I have found that the opposite can also be true. I did not want to move into the homeless shelter but the people there ended up being incredibly kind to me. They told me that I was welcome to stay as long as I needed. Under their care, I was able to get a new job and even start college!

The people who ran the shelter were saints. Unfortunately, some of the other people who lived there were not. The first time I was raped, I was thirteen years old. The second time happened at this homeless shelter. Both times, I experienced the same kind of disconnection between my mind and my body. To my horror and shame, both times, I froze.

When I realized that I was pregnant from the rape, the directors continued to embrace me. They walked through my pregnancy with me and even helped me find a safe apartment of my own. I appreciated their kindness, but my heart was bruised and broken again. I drifted away.

After my baby girl was born, I started working in a restaurant and later at a strip club called Girls. Once, I did try to do something different by working at the local chicken plant. I worked very long hours and my skin burned from the chemicals at the plant. When I was finally paid for the work, the check was so low, I was shocked. The amount was not even enough to feed my baby girl for one week! In desperation, I went back to Girls. There, I met Wilson, a gorilla pimp.

Wilson was another violent, dangerous man but he was much more professional than my son's daddy. Wilson moved into my apartment almost immediately. He said he didn't like the furniture so he had it moved into a storage container and replaced everything. He never told me where my things were but said he might give them back to me someday. He never did. Far worse, Wilson's family began providing child care to my daughter. The problem was, Wilson would always take her to them while I was "working." I had no idea where the family or my own daughter was! When it was time for me to see my daughter, it was Wilson who retrieved her. I lost control of every possession I had, including my baby daughter, in a matter of weeks.

One night, the U.S. Marshals came to our place looking for Wilson. I stalled while he quietly climbed out the window, but we knew they would be back. Wilson was on edge. One night I came home and heard Wilson whispering with my daughter. "Baby Girl tells me you have been seeing another man." This was laughable considering the work he was currently forcing me to do. Then he said, "Baby Girl, tell your mother goodbye. I'm going to end her life tonight."

It is hard to remember what happened next, except:

Screaming.
Ambulance lights.
A stretcher.

I know now that my sister, who wasn't even near our place that night, called the police and asked them to do a welfare check on me. She saved my life. The U.S. Marshals got their man while I lost custody of my daughter.

Free again and miraculously saved, but I was broken. I stopped caring. I thought about suicide many times, and even attempted it, but something kept me alive. When I met and fell in love with another man on the nation's Most Wanted List, it felt like home. When I ran tricks, Ben brought security; not only from dangerous clients but from Wilson himself. Ben knew where Wilson was in prison and his people made sure that Wilson left me alone. I finally felt safe. Then they arrested Ben. They kept me in jail for three weeks hoping that I would tell them something. When I didn't, they let me go but kept Ben. I was alone again. Online solicitation sites and prostitution were becoming an addiction for me. It made me sick and sad, but it was the only way I knew how to live.

Blake was my last pimp, and he was more dangerous than the others. He had a giant tattoo branded across my neck and trafficked me across the United States. Every day, we would run tricks and then drive at least an hour and a half to the next place. I got to the point where I no longer knew nor cared where I was. I had no feelings. After ten years of this life, I was numb.

Then one night, Homeland Security knocked on the hotel door. Lying completely naked on the bed, I snapped from my haze into acute terror. While other officers fanned around the room, removing the client and searching the premises, one man sat down with me and invited me to cover up. He looked me in the eyes, "What would your father think of what you are doing?"

I had no words. I missed my father. *What would he think?*

Then, he started talking about the Bible! "You see, Martha was busy doing all kinds of things but Mary, she sat at the feet of Jesus and He taught her how to live."

Mary and Martha
Father and daughter.
Husband and wife.
Pimp and...

My mind turned things over and over while he drove me to another homeless shelter. I felt the numbness beginning to return when he left me in the care of the shelter staff.

At the shelter, a woman of about 70 years invited me to sit down and relax. "Wait here," she said. She returned after about ten minutes carrying a large and heavy stock pot. "What's that for?" I asked, feeling slightly hungry at the sight. "I need to soak my feet," she said as she placed the pot on the floor. She looked me hard in the eyes. "Take off your shoes, dear." I removed my stilettos with unguarded suspicion. The

---

[6] Trick: committing an act of prostitution (from Shared Hope International at https://sharedhope.org)

old woman sat down on the floor, lifted my left foot and placed it in the warm water. When she reached for the other, I flinched. "What are you doing?" Locking her eyes into mine again, she placed my other foot in the warm, soapy water and began to rub the arches. "I'm here to wash your feet, Dear, like Jesus."

Tears betrayed me in big, swollen drops. She didn't even know me! She washed the dirtiest part of me! She felt the callouses and the blisters and remained completely un-phased. After so many years of feeling different, I finally felt accepted.

God brought many miracles into my life after that en-counter. Another time, I was facing prostitution charges from years before. I owed an enormous fine and possibly jail time. My probation officer accompanied me to my court hearing. As we waited, I began to cry. "I don't want to go back to jail. I won't make it with those people. I can't do it!" My rather large and serious probation officer stared back at me in silence awkwardly and then, after a minute said, "Well, how about we pray?" Dumbfounded, I bowed my head with him in the middle of the courtroom and joined him in prayer.

God got the charges dropped.

Finally, came the night when I loudly announced to the shelter prayer group that I would never, ever believe in Jesus until he gave me a sign. The man next to me started pray-ing for healing over the details of my life. He prayed about things I had not shared with anyone... private things. This was so unnerving that I literally ran from the room. The Holy Spirit, however, turned me around from inside out. I walked back into that room, a new woman of God.

It was my praying probation officer who actually rec-ommended The WellHouse. "Why would I want to go to Ala-bama?", I chided, arms folded. "There are people there who will listen to you", he said. So, I agreed to the trip. He was right; the people at The WellHouse listened. For the first time in my life, I was able to build a relationship with a Christian therapist who listened and helped and even laughed with me from time to time! If I could say one thing to a girl who decided to come to The WellHouse, it would be this:

Stay.

Stay as long as you possibly can. Healing is a long-term process. You will need lots of tools to overcome the pain that you have experienced. But with God, love, patience and the right people, anything is possible.

I am now a mother, a student, an employee, an alumna of The WellHouse, and a fully-committed, Bible-believing, ever-overcoming woman of God.

But you can just call me Grace.

A PART OF OUR PROCESS

*T*HE IMMEDIATE SHELTER (TIS). After stabilization and transitioning to The Immediate Shelter, while still battling fears and uncertainty, she begins to understand her victimization.

As she fights fear in the hard work of recovery, along the way, she comes to believe that she can. With her ongoing compassionate therapy and the possibility of reconciliation with children she thought she would never see again, she looks daily toward the hill to the apartments, which signify true healing. Hope has exploded in her whole being, and it shows in her whole countenance.

Then, she decides she wants to keep moving toward the life she was created to have.

This is a time of ongoing stabilization, and the therapeutic and crisis intervention skills utilized by the staff often play a stabilizing role so that the survivor is able to work on herself - not always an easy thing to do as it is easier to remain in pain than to address it at times.

Regaining important documents such as social security cards or birth certificates are major, tangible accomplishments during this time. She will also see the medical provider and receive needed medical treatment and medications as well as dental care. This is an important time in many ways, especially spiritually as she begins to experience God's love in action.

 She is growing.

KATE

Now the Lord is the Spirit, and where the Spirit of the Lord is, there is freedom. And we all, with unveiled face, beholding the glory of the Lord, are being transformed into the same image from one degree of glory to another. For this comes from the Lord who is the Spirit.

2 Corinthians 3:17–18

There is nothing like the grace and beauty of a stallion. The power of its gallop is exhilarating.

As a little girl, my mother made sure I took riding lessons. I always looked forward to our weekly journeys to the riding club outside of Washington DC.

My favorite horse was Major.

I remember when we had joined a new riding club, and Major had just arrived at the club and was settling into his new stall. Major was beautiful and big and powerful and was proving to be hard to handle. As much as trainers and club members tried, Major wouldn't let anyone ride him.

People grew afraid of him. And while others were afraid, I was both fascinated and drawn to him. So, I began spending time with Major in his stall. I would brush him, feed him, and talk to him. It wasn't long before I began to sense a bond.

One afternoon while brushing Major in his stall, I decided to put a saddle on him. After tightening the leather, I opened the stall door and climbed onto the saddle.

Suddenly, Major took off.

Clippety-clop.

I slipped and was hanging off the side of Major as we bolted out of the barn.

Clippety-clop. Clippety-clop.

I felt helpless under the force of such a powerful animal.

Clippety-clop. Clippety-clop. Clippety-clop.

While all this is unfolding, my mother was having a cup of tea on the veranda with a staff member of the club. As she lowered her teacup, she said to the staff person, "We are so thankful to have found this riding club. The staff is so safe here." The staff member looked over my mother's shoulder and saw Major running wild with her daughter dangling off his side.

Fortunately, no one was hurt. Major calmed down, and we all had a good laugh.

However, from that day on, Major and I had a bond. It has been said by some, "You don't choose your horse, but your horse chooses you." That was true for Major and me. I had been chosen. Because from that day forward, I rode Major several times a week. And that made me feel very special.

Born in 1961, I grew up with a lot of privileges. My parents were both graduates of Howard University. My childhood was filled with dance, ballet, and horses. We vacationed on Cape Cod on weekends and summers within eyesight of the Kennedy compound.

My parents always worked. Mom was a Vice-President of a multinational corporation. My father was an educator who also regularly volunteered in the community. While our family didn't live a perfect life, the house was always perfect. My parents insisted on it. The house had to be perfect, show-room perfect.

When I hit my high school years, I excelled academically. I was popular and had many friends. I wasn't into drugs, even though I knew people who were. Upon graduation, I was offered a scholarship to attend Tufts University.

Tufts gave me independence. My room no longer had to be perfect. I could put books on the floor and shoes under my bed. If I wanted to mess up my dorm room, I had the freedom to do so. By my sophomore year, I was beginning to make close friends.

Tufts had a free spirit that was contagious. And while I couldn't imagine how the future of my life might hinge on that reality, what began to unfold over the coming days would take me down a 26-year path of darkness and pain.

My friends were excited about spending a weekend in Chicago. They invited me to take part in the fun. When we arrived, we stayed in an upscale condo on Lakeshore Drive owned by one of their family members. As a group of college students all gathered in a condo for the weekend, friends and friends of their friends also joined us in the condo for a night of partying.

When I awoke the following morning, I was locked in one of the bedrooms. I kept questioning, "Why would a bedroom door be locked from the outside?" Confused and dazed by a late night of revelry and the unfamiliarity of it all, this is when I entered my personal hell.

My friends in Chicago gave me drugs, and I got hooked. And as I got hooked, one of these persons began to manipulate me. Slowly, over time, he groomed me into a life of prostitution. While at the time I didn't realize it, he became my pimp.

Under my pimp's influence, I was moved from state to state. In the coming years, there would not be a state in which I would not be trafficked.

Eventually, I ended up in jail for prostitution. Not long after my arrest, my parents found out and showed up to offer help and a way out. But my self-talk overruled their offer of help. "My parents don't really want me." Fear and shame governed my emotions and influenced my rejection of their love and offer of help. After all of the abuse I had suffered, I felt like a throwaway on the inside.

A few years later, while being trafficked in Las Vegas, I would be arrested again for prostitution.

I knew I had not been feeling well for some time, and deep down, I knew I was getting sick. After a series of tests, it was determined that I needed open-heart surgery.

While I was in the hospital, my pimp traded me to another pimp. In addition to the trauma of open-heart surgery, my heart navigated the pain of being treated like a commodity rather than a human being deserving dignity and value.

As I sat in the hospital room recovering from open-heart surgery, the doctor came in to check my vitals. While the doctor checked my pulse, my pimp came in, and the doctor noticed that my vital signs began to jump up.

I was nervous and unsettled, because my pimp didn't know that I was holding $7,200 in cash. After my pimp left, my doctor looked me in the eye and asked, "What's going on with you?"

Normally, I might have kept it all to myself. Maybe it was the pain meds. Or maybe my heart was too heavy. But I told the doctor my story. They immediately arranged for my security in the hospital. They even arranged a place for me to stay after I got out of the hospital.

After my recovery, I left Las Vegas and went to Kingston, Arizona. While there, I began to get sick again. It was during this time that I reconnected with Mom, but I still had an outstanding warrant. It was through being arrested and telling my story to law enforcement that I first had contact with The WellHouse.

This is when and where my healing process began. And the healing I needed was deep.

I was filled with anger.

I had been raped repeatedly.

I had been beaten repeatedly.

I had felt the weight of eight-and twelve-year-old girls

being trafficked around me.

I had been asked to recruit other girls into this nightmare.

I felt powerless as the anger raged within.

There were so many emotions to process: so much rage and pain.

My time at The WellHouse was not all easy. There were times when I wanted to leave. Yet, I am deeply grateful for what I learned from that place that helped me begin the process of healing.

During my time at The WellHouse, even as I felt close to members of the staff, I also was a bit of a loner. I tend to do this sometimes. But the solitude gave me time to read and reflect and process matters in a safe environment. The alone time was a healing balm.

Although challenging, I discovered more about forgiveness. While it's never easy to forgive people who hurt you, I grew to understand that forgiveness is about finding freedom in your own soul. And while forgiveness ultimately honors God, it also takes power away from the persons who have betrayed you and hurt you deeply. My heart grew freer from the prison of unforgiveness in the safe place that The WellHouse provided me.

Physical touch and presence can be powerful. A lot of healing came from the love I felt through hugs at The WellHouse and from the people at the church we attended on Sundays. As I healed, I also had opportunities to serve in ministry at that church.

I graduated from The WellHouse several years ago. Since that time, I am living a new life, one that is characterized by stability. In my former life, I saw a lot of money pass through the hands of people, but they didn't do anything meaningful with it. Today, I have a mortgage on my own home, pay my utility bills on time, and have an occasional evening out for a nice meal.

I love to paint, to crochet, and to arrange flowers. I have a growing relationship with my daughter and granddaughter. I cherish time with my family, especially time teaching my granddaughter how to ride a horse.

I believe God has given me a special ministry. On occasion, I go and minister at the homeless shelter. If I see someone in distress out in public, which is not hard to find these days, I will always spend time talking and listening to them. I remember, "I was that person." And I realize that by God's grace, my story may help someone else.

We don't always choose our story. But in the end, mine has been one of healing and hope. ✧

A PART OF OUR PROCESS

*E*QUINE AND ART THERAPY. Because each woman who enters The WellHouse is unique, we offer an array of creative, supplemental therapy opportunities.

The women at The WellHouse describe equine therapy as "soothing to the soul."

For this program, the women travel to a nearby horse farm staffed by trained equine therapy professionals. Here, the women care for the horses as they learn transferable lessons about life, grace, and the great outdoors.

Art therapy is a way some express their identity, story, and hopes. Experienced art instructors lead the program with the help of dedicated volunteers. Participants have created everything from vision boards to still-life paintings, from quilts to Christmas ornaments. Art therapy is a happy, hands-on activity at The WellHouse.

Not everyone loves working with horses and not everyone is an artist, but everyone seems to learn something from the experiences... and having some fun!

JOY

Oh give thanks to the Lord, for he is good,
   for his steadfast love endures forever!
Let the redeemed of the Lord say so,
   whom he has redeemed from trouble
and gathered in from the lands,
   from the east and from the west,
   from the north and from the south.

                                    –Psalm 107

I remember the silence afterward. Nobody wanted to talk about what had happened to me. I remember what I was wearing. I remember exactly where I was. I remember I was only four years old when my cousin molested me.

My mom knew immediately afterward, but still nobody talked about it. I was told that it shouldn't have happened and would never happen again. I don't remember much else, other than this is where my pain began.

I was raised in a rural, poor "Christian" family. I received a lot of love as the youngest of four children. Even as a young child, I remember believing that God was real. I had a very strong faith and deeply believed that God would take care of me. This faith has carried me through hell. In fact, I was probably more miserable while being trafficked because I knew deep down that I did not belong there. That God had created me for more.

Seven is my number.

But a defining tragedy struck when I was seven years old and in the first grade—my older brother, 12 years older than I, died of liver disease from substance abuse. Losing him on Mother's Day was especially hard on our family, and from then on, every Mother's Day was about him.

I often felt the hurt and pain in our family due to the death of my brother. My brother received a lot of attention both before his death and in death, and the family thought I was like him, even my laugh. At a young age, I began thinking that if I did what he did, I would receive the same attention that he got, so I moved away from my faith and the church at age 14.

Later, my Dad, who had been sober for ten years, began drinking alcohol again. Like Dr. Jekyll and Mr. Hyde, he transforms into a raging, alcoholic monster overnight. The alcohol abuse led to my parents beginning divorce proceedings.

By that point, I was so overlooked that when I decided to not go to school, nobody noticed. When my parents separated, I stayed with my dad while he abused alcohol. I simply could not bear to leave him alone, and my mom was so unwell that she allowed it.

When I was 16, out of the blue, my mother spoke of a cousin who had been molested. She looked at me and asked if anything ever happened to me.

I lost my breath.

I began hyperventilating.

This incident triggered my memory so badly that I began using drugs. Everyone was simply too tired to deal with me and the neglect continued. I was ashamed to invite my best friend over because our house was out of control due to my mom's depression.

My parents did not want me to spend the night away from home, but I felt so isolated at home with nothing to do.

Normal activities that other kids were doing were out of my reach, and at 16, I did something detrimental to my future – I quit school. I began using more drugs, and eventually when I tried to go back to school, it was too much of an uphill battle.

So, I was left to raise myself and lived a "gypsy" life of moving around from place to place, carrying my clothes and other belongings with me. Eventually, I reached age 20 and entered into my first real relationship which lasted until I was 25 when I broke off the engagement that we had.

I soon began dating another man which led to my first experience at being traded for sex. His coercion efforts led me to use cocaine, and eventually from being viewed as his girlfriend to his forcing me to become involved with another man, the drug dealer, and his partner. I was forced to be involved with them for drugs, and it soon became a routine. I hated doing it, but his typical line was, "if you love me", and so I continued. This happened for years.

I began to feel like I was running out of time to have a child, but I definitely did not want a baby with this man. One of my friends convinced me to go on a drug run at 3 a.m. It was then that I met the man who would become my son's father. It was a "love at first sight" experience, and I had butterflies immediately the first time I saw him.

The glimpse of sunlight in this dark time was that I did have a baby and settle down. I got out of all of it. Life was good for a minute. I did not do drugs during the pregnancy, and I knew I wanted a different life. After my son was born, I played around with drugs, but it was too much. Eventually, the father of my son became violent, and I had to leave and go to a safe house with my child. His mother reported me to family court for drug use, and the state's Child Protection Services agency took my baby.

I didn't know that a pickup order was issued that allowed my son's grandmother to have temporary custody of my child. So, when I went into the Police Department for safety from the father, my son was taken and given to the grandmother who had never kept him. I finally got custody back after 15 long months of working by a plan assigned to me by the state. I did everything they required.

I began working at a well-known and respected department store and became independent. I lived near my sister, had insurance and was actually happy. It seemed like God was raining blessings while I was doing the right thing. But, I became too relaxed because when the state stopped drug testing, then I started drinking wine – a little at first. I was still doing good, but I started dating someone – this has always seemed to be my downfall. These relationships brought out my weaknesses. I became too comfortable.

And then illness and grief struck our family.

My dad was diagnosed with dementia and died after several years in my sister's home. My mother was diagnosed with Lou Gherig's disease. During that time, I was not doing well coping with all of these heavy issues and I began using meth. I lost my great retail job after three-and-a-half years. I just stopped showing up for work. My relationships were affected, and I began not getting along with my sisters.

Our father died on New Year's Eve and my mother passed eleven months later.

I became separated from family members due to an incident that I am still unwilling to disclose. I was, once again, on my own, using alcohol, and I took advantage of each time my son stayed with his dad to do things not good for me. The people around me were not good people. I allowed someone to stay with me who used meth. An unexpected incident occurred with the burning of my home. I had spent all my money for living expenses, and a new dryer had been put into the home by someone who was intoxicated, and the dryer caught on fire and the home burned. Everything was lost.

My son was in 2nd grade, and I was desperate due to having lost everything. I moved to a friend's home, and my son's dad was in and out. I slid down a slippery slope and was kicked out of the home.

During this time, my son's dad and I got along, and I got along with his mother. But I texted the man who sold meth and became involved with him again. He became a trafficker to me and had me having sex for drugs and to pay rent.

To me, it was survival sex. But in reality, it was trafficking due to force, fraud, and coercion.

My life was threatened, so I called my son's dad. He told me to keep a ball bat by the door. He was looking to move closer to our son and he told me to check on some apartments in my small town the next day. We slept on my sister's couch that night. We thought there might be a little hope when tragedy struck. That night, my son's father had a heart attack.

The one person I always could depend on when it came to our son was gone. My life changed DRASTICALLY for the worst. My son lost his father but then would lose his mother also. My family stepped in immediately and took care of my son. Instead of focusing on my son losing the father he adored, I went straight for rock bottom as fast as I could go, continuing the life of drugs and sexual exploitation.

There is so much guilt and shame that I hold onto because of this decision.

Change came when my sister called the police. I had warrants for failing to appear in court. I remember becoming very angry at God and screaming at Him. I stayed 21 days in jail and while I was there, my sisters set up an entry into a program in Pennsylvania. I went there after leaving jail, and I did well there as it was small and there was much individual attention. However, they shut down their operation. A worker there got in touch with The WellHouse, and thankfully there was an open bed. They accepted me. It was around Thanksgiving, so I spent a week with my son before going to The WellHouse.

Even though I had been clean for six months and in another program, I was still required to enter The WellHouse in the first phase. This was disappointing to me, and I turned into a "negative Nancy" right away. Someone told me I was the most negative person in the room. I could not believe it and didn't understand why the staff of The WellHouse did not listen when I tried to tell them how they should run the program! And, I did not want to listen to them.

I was in a place where I could and I needed to work on issues of healing, but instead, I wanted to fight everything. Healing is hard work! And I had a lot of hard stuff to deal with. I had to deal with how I had gotten to this place in my life, and I had to do it without any self-love, a lot of shame and guilt, and so much pain. While I took some responsibility, the time came when I realized that no one deserves to be sold for any reason.

I often felt very alone and felt like I was the only one dealing with these issues. I felt very different from others. I still had not dealt with what had happened to me and I still wanted to pretend that I had actually had control over it all, but, freedom and healing began when I realized how badly I was victimized. My counselor at The WellHouse was very helpful during this time of deep soul-searching and realization.

I stayed in the first phase for a couple of months before moving to the second phase where I felt more acceptance. Maybe it was because I was in a better place with myself to be accepted. I had a wonderful roommate in this phase who I felt was led by God's spirit with much knowledge of God's work. This kept me grounded. Because we had a hard time finding a mentor for me, I found myself leaning on God even more. God gave me a perfect formula of gifts to help me become stronger. I embraced my recovery program, and I had an opportunity to go to college. There were some failures which kept me praying continuously.

Then.....we were told that we had to move! The entire organization was moving to a new location. I saw the enemy attacking us all, from the leadership down to the residents, but God allowed miracle after miracle. It was wonderful for all of us to have experienced the real hand of God during that time. I truly felt that I was in the right place at the right time.

The move was an adjustment for us all. We did not like people coming to see our new home, but, a turning point was when we, the residents and I, said that we were going to focus on why we were at The WellHouse. I truly surrendered during this time. Something transformational happened! It was a complete turnaround with the way I looked at things. I surrendered to God to be at The WellHouse as long as He wanted me to be. I began working. At one time I was working three jobs, but I constantly felt God's spirit and strength. People told me they could see God's spirit on me, and it was so real! Still I had disappointment after disappointment during this time. I had even planned to leave The WellHouse a year earlier, but God knew I needed that extra year! I remain so very grateful for that year. Even the long bus ride to church was an opportunity to reflect. To think that those people drove all the way out there to pick us up was amazing.

The last year at The WellHouse was a year of prayers prayed and prayers answered! I saved more money than I had ever saved in my life. I remember when I had to go to court for the custody issue surrounding my son. My sister still had custody and I was not fighting her – I just wanted more of my son's time. And, God answered that prayer. But, what I really recall is that the day of court was my case manager's birthday and that she chose to go to court with me.

God gave me everything. He ordained things so perfectly. I was able to get an apartment near my sister and my son, and right before I left The WellHouse, a friend called and told me about a job nearby. I still have that job several years later.

Seven is my number.

God gave me a home seven miles from my son's school and seven miles from my sister. When my son started staying with me, my sister was receiving his social security from his dad, and I did not want to ask her for it. But she volunteered to give it to me. They were receiving $748, but when I began the process for the check to come to me, the Social Security department sent me a letter that they were raising the amount to $777! Another of many signs from God that I am His and He will forever take care of me!

Today, I am active with my family; I see them often. We talk daily, and life is good. I am stable with a good job as a dependable employee. People love me, and my son just graduated from high school. Most importantly my son loves and knows he can trust his mother to do the next right thing. We don't look back at bad memories; we just constantly appreciate the new ones that we make, and we try to live in the present. Now, I love myself more than I ever have. And it's just me and my son at this time of life. What a gift! God is good.

God has been my mentor. And joyfully, I know He will be with me through it all.

A PART OF OUR PROCESS

*C*ARING FOR SOULS.
The level of betrayal she has experienced prior to The WellHouse is enough to destroy her trust in people, institutions, and even God.

Sensitive to this, The WellHouse is committed to providing an environment of prayer, excellence, and grace to each survivor. Our staff prays continually and offers prayer to residents whenever needed.

We seek out the excellence in every woman as a reflection of our glorious God while remembering that He is gracious and kind, slow to anger, and abounding in steadfast love.

Women who were lonely, lost, and broken were at the very heart of the ministry of Jesus. Reflecting on his gentleness and grace with which He handled people's deepest pains, we seek to embody his care for broken people to be made whole.

And she is on her journey toward that wholeness.

RUTH

Remember that you were at that time separated from Christ, alienated from the commonwealth of Israel and strangers to the covenants of promise, having no hope and without God in the world. But now in Christ Jesus you who once were far off have been brought near by the blood of Christ.

Ephesians 2:12–22

I am resilient.

Which is good, because resilience was key to my survival and ultimate recovery. Despite many setbacks stemming from painful childhood experiences, I believe I embody a God-given resilience that changed the outcome of my life's story.

In my younger years, I had a decent childhood. But, at age six, it came to light that my dad molested my sisters, his stepdaughters, and, at that time, I did not know what that meant. My dad was 53 when I was born, and he already had six children. He had abandoned his other family when he met my mom, continuing a family cycle of brokenness.

As a result of this horrific, abusive behavior from my dad, my mom attempted suicide. I later understood that her own experience of childhood molestation had triggered her distress and her ultimate suicide attempt. My mom ended up in a psychiatric ward for, what seemed like, a long time. She was so broken when she realized that she had entered a relationship with a predator. She eventually left my dad, not knowing what else to do. Leaving my dad was a great loss to me, especially since no one really explained to me what was going on.

We moved from the Northwest to a trailer park in the Deep South.

When I was seven, my sister's husband molested me. I was 12 before I understood what had happened. He had also molested a neighbor child. This was the beginning of my sexual objectification by men, an early age to be experiencing such atrocities that would impact me for a lifetime.

Even after my mom remarried and eventually told me what my dad had done to my sisters, my dad was still in my life. So, I bounced back and forth from the Northwest to the South. Of all the children between the marriages, I was the youngest. Some of my siblings were even old enough to be my parents.

My Mom battled deep anger, and never quite won that battle. I was mad at her because she did not know how to protect us. She loved us, but she was so broken herself. When she felt like she failed, there would be suicide attempts.

My dad gave his life to Christ after he met my stepmom, and even admitted what he had done. My stepmom also led me to Christ at age 13. However, my mom's anger had skewed my mind from a young age. Even though I had accepted Christ's offer of salvation, I was not in a growing relationship with Christ until I was much older. My mom's vacillating love and hatred toward God made it difficult for me to trust. My mom knew He was God, but she could not understand why He allowed everything to happen as it did. The ongoing dysfunction in my home made it very challenging to exercise true faith.

As a teen, I started manipulating people. I learned how to manipulate my mom to get my way. These survival skills were dysfunctional and followed me into adulthood.

Miraculously, I graduated from high school. I was the only person to do so in the family.

After my mom died of cancer when I was 19, I clung to my boyfriend and married him. He was addicted to drugs, and up until then, I had not really done drugs. But, the pain was so great for me, that I sought relief through drug abuse.

Eventually, I had a son. I moved back to the Northwest to rekindle a relationship with my dad and began working with him. I was able to gain custody of my nieces due to my sister's addiction. But, parenting a teen and then being in a car accident myself with my son when he was two years old left me far more stressed than I should have been.

While I was not prepared to take on my nieces, there was no one else, but I could not adequately meet their needs, and was left feeling very alone and isolated. After the accident I relapsed on pain pills. I also had to have more surgery to repair my ankle. I had no support system to speak of and it was easy to rely on pain pills to take away all feeling. I justified it because of my circumstances. It felt good to not feel anything, to be numb

Yet I still chose this path. There is no excuse, but those were the reasons. My feelings were not wrong, but the way that I chose to cope was wrong. I did not want to be dependent on drugs because that was my sister's issue, and I was trying to protect my nieces from it. But, I just kept on.

Without a relationship with my dad and then the loss of my mom, the pain just became too much to handle. In addition to my losses with my parents, one of my sisters was in a serious car accident, one began practicing witchcraft, and one sister died in 2014 with my biological dad.

It was too much pain to bear!

I packed up and moved south again and left my nieces with a family friend. I had completely relapsed on drugs, including meth this time. I do not know what I was thinking. I thought I would have more support, but that was not the case. I was not close to my dad's family because I was the reminder of his sins.

I turned to others who were not good influences. I relapsed on meth for a year, and my son was taken from me. At this time, sexual exploitation became a part of my life which only fueled the guilt, shame, and drug use. My son went into foster care until we established paternity and he could go to his dad's parents. I was left alone with nothing but the endless cycle of substance use and the trauma of sexual exploitation from those who simply did not care if I lived or died.

I tried to get mental health assistance, but no one would help me. I was on the phone with one facility for three-and-a-half hours, and they told me that I could not receive help unless it was court-ordered. Only after committing a felony and going to jail was I able to get help. The felony was a charge of fraudulent use of a credit card and the guy who had the card was the trafficker, but I used it. Thankfully, I went to jail, because it was while I was in jail that I cried out to God.

I had nowhere to go but to Him. So, I cried out hoping He would hear me and help me. I told Him that He was going to have to help me and provide me with a completely new environment so I could break the horrible patterns that enslaved me, including the drugs and sexual exploitation that had eaten away at my very being.

Abusing drugs is bad enough. It just adds to the pain that a person is trying to relieve. But, when a human being is being sold by and to another human being, a layer of trauma is added that requires a God-sized miracle to overcome. Fortunately, I was about to experience one!

While I was in jail, my son's step-grandmother had heard the founder of The WellHouse speak at an event. So, I got out of jail and Susan, my son's step-grandmother, sent me the number for The WellHouse and they came and got me – that quickly! I called the number on a Tuesday, talked to the Rescue Supervisor, and the Rescue Supervisor got me the next day on a Wednesday.

I didn't even know The WellHouse or places like The WellHouse existed. People did not talk about trafficking during this time very much. But, I walked onto the porch of The WellHouse with the intention of staying no longer than 30 days. Then the staff convinced me to stay 60 days. Then everything changed. I knew I needed help and I needed love, and I really felt loved at The WellHouse. It was genuine! They pretty much had to push me out to get me to leave. I never wanted to be alone again.

To get my son back I had to go through court ordered treatment facilitated by the state's CPS department, which included taking anger management classes. The WellHouse offered all of the required services and they helped me to get through all of those requirements. What happened through The WellHouse was essentially the rebuilding of a completely new foundation.

I completed the required classes, which The WellHouse offered to me, along with the consistency and support of key relationships. They were so committed to me and my success. The State came to The WellHouse and visited a few times. Gradually, visitation began with my son which progressed to weekend visitation. This also served to motivate others to do what they needed to do as they watched me achieve goals. Eventually, I was awarded back custody of my son. This was the greatest highlight of my time and journey with The WellHouse and this has been a chief motivator for me to continue on the right path.

I was very fortunate to have realized a dream of enrolling in college, and received a scholarship through Safe Port Initiative for some college classes. I went through WorkFaith, a jobs skills program, and obtained employment with their assistance. There are many people in recovery working in the business I am in, and I have decided that I can gradually learn how to broker for this company and make this my career. Perseverance in my college classes helped me to move forward on this path!

The WellHouse provided me with the tools I would need to leave and become a successful mother, and a functioning and a productive member of society, as well as a Christian that is now connected to a thriving body of Christ. Things I never thought I'd ever accomplish or become have come true, and I left The WellHouse a totally different person than when I arrived. I had people who loved me well while I was there and people who actually really believed in me way more than I believed in myself. I thought I was dealt my lot in life that I would have to work with forever. That was completely false. I now have a family of people who truly love both my son and me and that has made all of the difference in the world. I worked my program. I made small goals at first then took the steps to achieve those goals, such as the tremendous life-changing goal of getting custody back of my son. Then, working to save money for a car while planning for a move to my own place became achievable goals. All of this happened through knowing people I met through The WellHouse and networking. God knew what He was doing the whole time.

I am learning that I have the power through Christ who changed my heart to make my life and my son's life whatever I want it to be. I make enough money to support my son and me. I am extremely grateful to The WellHouse for always loving both my son and me even when I haven't been the most receptive or loving person myself.

Life is full! As a final chapter to my story, I am now engaged to be married to a wonderful man who loves me and my son as his own. Truly, the ending is far greater than the beginning in my life's story. And I can't wait for the next chapter.

A PART OF OUR PROCESS

*N*EXT STEPS TO FREEDOM. She and her Case Manager develop a plan just for her. It may include:

- regaining custody of a child
- graduating with a GED or going to college
- a certain career path
- or her newfound faith!

A glance back at her first arrival reveals noticeable change. She completes her goals, one by one, with some occasional steps backward. At that time, those surrounding her catch her and bring her back. A brave, new life evolves. Many, including a dedicated mentor, pray for her, love her well, and extend grace, all of which help her stay on the path of healing.

During this time, she prepares for her exit from NSF to transitional living in the apartments. The Case Manager ensures she is ready to move forward either into one of our Transitional Living apartments or another exit plan. She is able to regain or obtain a driver's license, and due to the generosity of WellHouse donors, she is able to receive matching funding in order to purchase a vehicle, sometimes the first she has ever owned. She obtains employment as she continues to complete her education, allowing her to obtain more sustainable employment.

She is achieving her goals.

EDEN

They shall see the glory of the Lord,
  the majesty of our God.
Strengthen the weak hands,
  and make firm the feeble knees.
Say to those who have an anxious heart,
  "Be strong; fear not!
Behold, your God
  will come with vengeance,
with the recompense of God.
  He will come and save you."

–Psalm 35

remember going to therapy when I was in middle school. I know they tried to help my sister and I, but we didn't understand. We thought everyone was just like us. My twin sister and I grew up in what I now know was a "challenging environment."

We loved school. We loved getting on the school bus each morning, talking to the other kids and even the bus driver. We loved our classes, our books, and our school supplies. However, when the school day was over and we rode the bus home, we experienced terrible stomach aches. A wave of anxiety came over us each time. We knew we needed a safe space, but we didn't know where to find one. When the bus reached our house every afternoon, we knew our mother was close behind.

She was a teacher. But, she wielded a wooden paddle with strength and conviction as she punished us for any number of incomprehensible infractions. If our language was unacceptable, there was the bar of soap. Except, washing our mouth out with it wasn't enough. With Mom, you ate the entire bar. If we threw up, she made us eat our own vomit off of the floor. I remember one time Mom forced my sister and I into a scalding hot shower. That was the only time my father ever intervened. I have always appreciated him for doing that. I never forgot.

I remember the day my sister and I were called to the school nurse's office. We were asked to remove our clothing and allow pictures to be taken of our bodies. The next memory is of my mother, crying and screaming, "You did this to me! This is all your fault!" Then, people removed my sister from our home. I had to stay with my mother. Finally, they settled both of us with our Aunt and Uncle, which was a much safer environment.

Life took on a calmer, more predictable feeling after that. I tried to focus on school and friendships, but I had a lot of trouble managing life. I enjoyed school more than ever, but memories of the abuse would flood my mind, making it difficult to concentrate, and almost impossible to build healthy friendships. Isolation and rebellion felt like the most comfortable responses to my feelings. Unfortunately, something terrible happened.

At the age of fifteen, someone raped me. I woke up after a night of partying and the first thing I saw was the blood. It was all over me. My body stung from the violent assault. I was shocked, horrified, and filled with shame. In my mind, my mother told me that the rape was my fault. It was what I deserved.

I carried my dual existence into adulthood. Part of me loved learning and loved people. The other part was flooded with fear and pain. I married, completed my nursing degree, began a career, and had two beautiful babies, a boy and a girl. But I also battled depression, insecurity, and a strong desire to end my life. During those days, I attempted suicide multiple times. I took any pill that I could find to numb the pain that I was feeling inside. I know now that I was a perfect candidate for a trafficker.

I met my trafficker through a friend at the hospital where I worked. She told me I would really enjoy hanging out with her brother, and honestly, she was right. She introduced us one night after work. He made me laugh in a way that helped me forget my fear, if even for a moment. I thought he was funny and found myself attracted to him almost immediately. We laughed and talked and drank a ridiculous amount of alcohol that first night. I felt free. I woke up the next morning realizing that I never went home to my family and that I was in bed with this new man.

Before I was able to figure out my next step, my friend, bothered by the events of the previous night, phoned my husband. He was furious and demanded that I leave our home and family. It may sound strange that I agreed to leave my husband and children, but I was not a healthy person at the time and we both knew it. What judge would possibly give me, a woman with multiple recent suicide attempts, custody of her children? I did the only thing that felt right at the time. I stayed with my new man, Frank. I already felt a kinship with him. Actually, I was already in love. Frank took me in when I was at my lowest point. I called him my "Knight in Shining Armor". He turned out to be the devil.

Very early into our relationship, Frank introduced me to methamphetamines. The first time I tried them, I had a strong and strange reaction. I took the drug and "woke up" outside, pacing and screaming. No matter how I tried, I could not calm myself down. Eventually, the paramedics were called. From my bed at the ER, I felt someone familiar touch my hand. I opened my eyes to find my sister by my side. Also a nurse, she held my hand and warned me that I was headed down a dark and dangerous path. I loved my twin sister more than anyone in the world, but when the hospital released me, I went right back to Frank.

He had a violent side. I soon learned that Frank had served several prison sentences for beating other women. He hit, punched, and knocked me down on the regular. Once, Frank shot me with a rifle designed for deer hunting.

Somehow, I survived. But why did I stay? The only reason I can think of is that I was searching for love and strangely, Frank's abuse felt like home. His temper continued to escalate, though. Before long, I was just trying to survive.

The first time Frank demanded I have sex with another man for money, I was too afraid to say no. When it happened, I noticed that I didn't feel the terror of my mother's abuse. I didn't feel the pain or shame of the rape. I felt nothing. I felt like a dead body. This sensation of disconnection and death was enough to carry me through the multiple men who paid Frank to have sex with me over and over again.

Frank controlled everything I did: where I went, when I slept, and what I ate. He would feed me little, tiny pieces of food just to keep me going. One day, Frank decided we were moving to Mississippi. I was stunned by how quickly he packed all of his things and put them in a bag. He put my clothes into a pile and set them on fire. He threw my driver's license and any papers with my name on them into the burning heap. I watched while every trace of me was burned into nothingness.

When we arrived in Georgia, Frank took me to a quiet, open space. Then, he began digging a hole. When it was complete, he looked at me and said, "This is where I will bury your body if you ever disobey me." This was the beginning of our trafficking pilgrimage from state to state.

Every time, he hastily packed a bag.
Every time, he set my things on fire.
Every time, he threatened death.

I managed to stay alive by the grace of God. I did the best I could to support our household. At one point, we agreed that I should also work at a nursing home during the day. Already exhausted, I wondered how I would have the strength to begin a day job in addition to my nighttime sex quota. To my surprise, the nursing home became a place of peace for me. I made friends easily with the elderly residents and enjoyed the simplicity of their stories of home and family. Frank picked up on my growing affection for the place and the people there. He became increasingly irritated and angry.

One day, he went too far. In a rage, no doubt fueled by any mixture of illegal substances and years of dominating, dangerous behavior, Frank attacked me in the parking lot of the nursing home. He grabbed me hard and dragged me, screaming into his automobile. What Frank did not know was that two of my coworkers witnessed the incident and called the police. When they were able to find us in a local hotel room, Frank had me pinned to the ground, choking, unable to breath. If the police had been five minutes later, I would have died. Thankfully, Frank was sent to prison for what he did. I was free.

I'd like to say that coming home again felt great. True, it was very good to be free from my trafficker. I reconnected with my sister and had some hope for a new life. It was difficult, though. I was safe on the outside but inwardly, I felt chaotic. Now addicted to meth, it dominated my life. I couldn't function without it. Alcohol was one of the only things that brought me back down afterwards. One night, I found myself at a local bar doing shots of tequila. Feeling pretty good, I pounded shot after shot. Then, driving home, I saw the blue lights behind me and heard the siren. They sent me to jail that night with a DUI. I spent 94 days incarcerated.

People don't always tell you this but jail can save your life. Detox was far from easy but I had no other choice. Jail was also the place where I met one of the most important people in my life. She introduced herself to me as a participant in a ministry for trafficked women. She helped me see that my strongest, truest healing could only come from God. She also told me about The WellHouse, a residential program that helped women like me rebuild their lives. I knew that mine was out of control. I agreed to let her take me to Alabama, and I joined the program.

The WellHouse is a beautiful place in the middle of nowhere. I looked around and the hills and the pond and began to feel my racing anxiety begin to calm. I met the Home Coordinator who lived with the ladies. She was kind and gentle with me. For the first time in my life, I sensed the Spirit of God around me. I remembered a time when I was eleven years old that I attended a Billy Graham crusade. At that young age, I walked down the stadium steps to be with the crowd on the field below. There, eleven year old me, during the height of my mother's abuse, asked Jesus to be my Savior.

He never forgot me.

At The WellHouse, I fully dedicated my life to him. I found my new identity in Jesus. No longer abused or threatened or tortured, I am a child of the King. I am an heir of the Kingdom. Looking back on my time at The WellHouse, I wish I had stayed longer. Sometimes you don't know a pivotal point in your life until it has already happened. After almost a year, I returned to my hometown.

The transition back to my city was not easy. Memories and people from my past seem to be lurking around every corner. Even though I try to put it in the back of my mind, there are triggers. There are smells and sounds that bring me back. But God keeps me safe. He told me, "You're not done. You're going to keep walking this road, and you're going to be strong. You're going to use the things you have learned."

He introduced me to a wonderful, Christian man who has become my husband. Together, we have joined a local church. We are both working full time jobs and recently purchased a home. I even have a mother-in-law! To me, she is my new mother. The memories of my childhood still haunt me sometimes, but now I have the courage to press on. I am proud of the woman I am becoming. ✧

A PART OF OUR PROCESS

*L*IFE SKILLS & EMPLOYMENT. Life skills and employment are a critical part of The WellHouse way. Each woman is encouraged to set specific goals and objectives for her life.

Resumé building, interview training, certifications, formal education, computer skills, financial management, and a host of other opportunities help people tackle the real-life challenges that come with independent living.

To accomplish this level of life skill training, The WellHouse combines our in-house curriculum with the expertise of several committed community partners.

She is hopeful.

HOPE

As a deer pants for flowing streams,
    so pants my soul for you, O God.
My soul thirsts for God,
    for the living God.
When shall I come and appear before God?
My tears have been my food
    day and night,
while they say to me all the day long,
"Where is your God?"
These things I remember,
    as I pour out my soul:
how I would go with the throng
    and lead them in procession to the house of God
with glad shouts and songs of praise,
    a multitude keeping festival.

–Revelation 21:4-5

As a child, I remember that I loved to play outside and I always did well in school. It was my escape from my home life, a distraction for my mind.

I had been adopted as a baby, but my adoptive parents got divorced when I was three. My mom got remarried when I was six. The first time I remember my stepdad being verbally abusive was when I was nine years old. I remember during the formative ages of 9–16 that the verbal abuse contained sexually-charged comments. By the time I turned 11, I was interested in becoming sexually active. I never had a lot of friends, but I started hanging out with a lot of boys and smoking pot.

My mom smoked pot every day, too., although she didn't condone me smoking pot. I always thought it was hypocritical... like you shouldn't do this, but I am going to.

I always wanted my older sister's attention. I wanted her to like me and approve of me, but being three years older than me, she had no interest in me. She had a tight relationship with my mom. When she started getting into trouble, I was around 11 years old, and a lot of attention in the house was being given to her punishment and her rebellion. My stepdad would get in her face and yell, and both my mom and I would stand between them to protect my sister. She got older, and I got older, and then I started to act out too.

I started working when I was 12 at the community center. I also did improv acting, which was fun, kept me busy, and kept me away from my house as much as possible. When I started to become interested in boys and getting in a little bit of trouble, my mom didn't want to deal with it anymore, and when I tried to talk to her about boys, she'd call in my stepdad to talk to me. He functioned as my main parent, but I was scared of him.

My adoptive dad was across the country taking care of his mom, and he was also an addict. I barely saw him at all from ages 10-17, but looking back now, I know he was high all the time.

The abuse from my stepdad turned from verbal to physical to sexual. He would tell me things like "I don't know what I want and I don't know what I need." I knew inherently that something was wrong, and I was doing my best, but no one was listening to me. I would tell my mom "I'm scared of this man," but she would tell me to stop being so dramatic or to put on more clothes. I think she knew what was going on, but she just didn't want to deal with it. I was still scared to go home, but I didn't really have a choice. My behavior when acting out was a response to the abuse, but it actually hurt me more. It was a cycle. Because of the abuse, I internalized that sex was the only way to make people like me. It became the same with my traffickers...

My stepdad would abuse me, then he felt really bad, so he would show me love and be pleasant with me. I could ask for anything and he would give it to me because of his guilt. This dynamic continued into every subsequent relationship I had. There was a bond that took place because of all the attention I was getting and because my mom ignored me completely and didn't want anything to do with me. To me, bad attention was better than no attention. I wanted to feel loved, important, special... something every child should feel. Even though I was raised as a Christian in church, I didn't have Jesus in my heart.

Instead, I started hanging out with older people and drinking when I was 13, and then all throughout high school. I lost my virginity at 13. Sex and sex culture completely shaped my life. With drugs and alcohol involved, there's no way I could see clearly. I didn't want to see, because that would have meant facing the truth about my stepdad and my own worth and value.

I started going to college in Colorado and was on my own. My first experience with trafficking was here when I was 19. I worked at a restaurant as a prep cook, working my tail off 6 days a week, eventually working my way up to catering manager. I worked dine-in and catering on salary. If I worked anything over 40 hours a week, then my boss, Gary, would pay me cash under the table. I got cash Christmas bonuses too. Gary knew people in high places and in high standing, like lawyers, police officers, and judges. My other job for Gary outside the restaurant was cleaning houses. He would set me up with his friends to clean their houses, but I would clean and then have sex with those clients. Sometimes I wouldn't clean the house at all, or I would do it naked. I'd sit and drink with them, and they'd touch me.

Gary took advantage of me. I see it now but didn't then. I felt special, needed, and I liked the free alcohol. Alcohol has always been my way of coping. Although I did get paid for cleaning, I was naïve.

Soon, I got into real trouble. I got two DUIs and started dating a much older man. I was 22 and he was a 40 year old thief. I got into hardcore drugs, including methamphetamines. This man would pay me to spend time with him and do drugs with him. Knowing I was going to go to jail for my second DUI, I fled as a felony fugitive to the state of Georgia.

That's where I started living in hotels and getting into

harder drugs like cocaine and crack. For a while I was working at a chain restaurant, feeling like I was just partying and living my care-free lifestyle. I continued to see older men who would solicit me from my restaurant job. They would pay to spend time in my hotel room for sex. At this point, it was just me... I didn't have a trafficker; I was just doing that myself.

Some of the guys thought that they were in love with me. I lived with different guys and worked at different restaurants. One of my managers would eventually become a client. At this point, I wasn't walking the streets.

I met Spencer, had sex with him, and got pregnant. I had this idea that I could have a family, things can settle down, and life could be better. Spencer proposed when I was 8 months pregnant. We got married and bought a house. He was ready, but I wasn't. After I got done breastfeeding, I started drinking again, and then having marital issues with Spencer. I met Angelo and fell head over heels in love with him. He is the one who took me away from my family.

I remember in the beginning with Angelo, I would talk about my family a lot. I'd cry about it, obsess about it. But the next thing I remember I woke up somewhere else. I'm not sure if I fell asleep in the car or what happened, but he drove me away to another city. And he taught me everything I needed to know.

He taught me how to walk down the street, how to price, how to steal from people, and he was always right behind me on foot or in the car. He regulated me. If I didn't act right, he'd slap me. He played a lot of mind games with me. He would invite me to his mom's house for dinner and tell his mom that I was his girlfriend. I really thought I was his girlfriend and he loved me. And the next day I'd be right back out on the streets.

I wanted to drink and get high a lot. I don't know if I liked the attention or the money. A couple of times Angelo lost me and couldn't find me. I got knocked out and got raped, and it took him days to find me. I didn't even know where I was at that point. I was living out of hotels and my car, and every bit of my money went to him. I wanted to give it to him. He was taking care of me, and I thought he loved me. I really did.

Then, I got caught in an online prostitution sting. They got me and 13 other girls. Instead of taking me to jail, they questioned me and tried to get me to tell them about my trafficker. I didn't turn him over at all. This was my first prostitution charge. I was able to get out the next day. I had a first court appearance, and since this was my first prostitution charge it was a misdemeanor, and they let me go with the promise of showing up again in court.

After that, Angelo and I got into a really bad fight one night. He left the hotel room, and I left and deliberately walked down the wrong street. In that city, there are some really unsafe streets, ones that you just don't walk down as a female in the middle of the night. I ran into three known drug dealers and traffickers, and they proceeded to rape me for about 7 hours, taking turns. The next day, Angelo sold me to them for a car.

Somehow, I convinced those guys to let me go to my hotel room so I could get clothes. In the process, somebody called the cops. I am not sure whether it was Angelo or my parents. But when I got to the hotel the cops showed up. One of the drug dealers was with me to keep an eye on me and keep me in check. But he was too scared to leave the hotel room since the cops were out there. I was like, "I'm a grown woman and an adult, I'm not scared of the cops or of these guys, I'm taking the chance" and I just grabbed my stuff and I left and walked right past the cops. I hitchhiked back across the state.

But... I quickly ran into another trafficker. His name was Rob, and he was good to me until he wasn't. He had me doing drugs, and then he got me pregnant. When I told him, he refused to take care of me or help me out. I wasn't submissive enough and wasn't making enough money. So then, I was on the streets, pregnant and alone, still trying to stay afloat. But I was hungry. I got really upset and decided to hitchhike back across the state again. I laughed at the situation I was in...

When I had been with Angelo, I met a guy named JC, which was why I decided to hitchhike back. JC had a decent house so I knew I could at least have a place to stay with him. He knew I was pregnant and never wanted me to work the streets. He did not have pure intentions, but he didn't want me to work the streets. He just wanted me to take care of him with cooking and cleaning and sex. I figured it was better than the alternative. A few weeks into being there at his house though, I did go out to go to work and I got caught in a sting by getting in the wrong car with a guy who was helping the cops.

I was arrested, but for the first time, I was actually grateful to be arrested because I was pregnant. It was my second prostitution charge, but I also had cocaine on me. So I was charged with possession and prostitution. I was able to get deferred adjudication and not be charged as a felon. But 45 days in to being in jail, I miscarried at 6 months gestation. I went to the hospital under a pseudonym, was cuffed to the hospital bed, and gave birth to a stillborn baby six hours later. He was a beautiful baby boy.

17 days after that I got out of jail and my parents came to pick me up. I went to rehab and was doing well after a little bit. I thought I had it all together. After two weeks I checked myself out, thinking that I was okay. I just wanted to see my daughter, because I felt guilty that I had abandoned her. But, that night, I went right back out. I met up with one of my Johns who I had met through Rob and was getting high on crack and alcohol that night.

I was easily drinking a fifth of vodka a day by myself. I worked the streets by myself for a few weeks. There was one street—30th street—that Angelo always told me to never walk down. One day I decided... I'm gonna stroll down there.

There was this tall, gated house, obviously locked up with a trailer and cabins in the back. It was a whole piece of property gated all the way around and had security cameras everywhere. There was a guy standing out front and I asked him for a cigarette. His name was Terry from Trinidad. Terry ended up being not so friendly.

At first, I would come in the house with him and hang out and drink, and he would buy me drugs. The second time I was there, an older woman named Gina walked into the house looking me up and down. She asked me to do drugs with her to be sure I wasn't a cop and I agreed.

I learned later that Gina was his bottom[7] and Terry was the pimp. They had a twisted relationship and they reeled me in. He would make it seem like he didn't want me to prostitute, but he would punish me by beating me. I was not allowed to have a phone and I could only leave when he let me out. I could climb the gate, but he would see me on the security cameras. He wanted me for himself, said he loved me, and that he had never met anybody like me. Terry was an electrician and worked for a living, but he and Gina had a deal going on. She was the one who would put me to work.

She practiced voodoo. There was dark magic there. No matter where I went, they knew where I was. They could always find me. It seemed like only Gina could get me out of trouble, but they would keep me in trouble if I crossed a line. I would give my money to her. She would call the cops, and he would bail me out. And I would be forever obligated to them.

---

[7] Bottom: a female appointed by the trafficker to supervise others and report rules violations. (From the Maryland Human Trafficking Task Force)

Somehow I felt like I had a home, but I was also terrified for my life. Gina lived in one of the cabins, and I lived in the house with Terry. They would hog tie me and beat the hell out of me. In the two years I was with him, I had nine broken bones- cheekbone, fingers, and almost my jaw. I was covered in bruises but would never call the cops. I would go to the fire station a couple blocks up and stay long enough till they started asking questions, and then I would haul ass.

I don't know why, but I had a loyalty to Terry like I never had to any other traffickers. And to Gina too. I was always conflicted, confused, and drunk. They always gave me liquor, because I would get sick if I didn't have it. He played mind games with me.

One time he slung my head into a car window. But then he would say, "I love you. I want better for you. I want you to be able to go back to your family." Later he would say, "You can never go back to your family. You know they're better off without you." I wanted to be a good person and a good mother, but I was high and drinking. If Terry was beating me, sometimes Gina would come in and say "you can't put your hands on her," then drag me out to the sidewalk and beat me up herself. Or I would be walking the sidewalk, Gina would tell him I was walking the streets, then Terry would pull up and tap me with the bumper of the truck until I got in. The mind games were ceaseless.

No matter what happened the cops seemed to never touch him. One fight was especially bad. I walked in the room and Gina was all over Terry, so I flipped out. I grabbed her to get her off, and she began strangling me. I pushed her, and I didn't have a weapon so she must have fallen into a metal bed frame with a gash on her head. I didn't know she was bleeding but she pushed me into the ground, she kicked me in the face, and then I started bleeding. Terry was just sitting there watching. I remember looking at him a few times through the whole thing and seeing him smiling. I couldn't help thinking that this is what he wants. I ran to the fire station and didn't want to go back there for the whole night. But I did end up coming back, and with some money. When I arrived, she was leaving in a foam neck brace in an ambulance. She pressed charges against me for aggravated assault. Terry was just standing right there and saw the whole thing.

He got an injunction against me, and Gina got me banned from the property. Even though I got mail there too, Terry would say that I did not live there. I lived in fear of all the charges, the upcoming court cases, and for my very life. I can't even remember exactly what it was... you think something I had been through would have been enough to get my attention and get out of there. All of the times I was in and out of jail, everything became too much. Something in my spirit cracked. I was mad, livid, upset, but I couldn't get out because they had locked me in. I didn't feel like hopping the fence and getting beat up. I was terrified and hated my life. I missed my family, my daughter, and the life I never had. I wanted peace. My spirit broke.

Instead of hurting myself or someone else I started breaking my own things. I broke my mirror and whatever I could in order to upset Gina. And it worked. She called the cops on me. It was a breaking point and that was it. I got arrested.

I wasn't sure about fighting the case although I could have. The regular public defender was not an option for me though. Gina had been an informant in a murder case years before, and they were her public defender so I couldn't use them because of conflict of interest. So I had to get outside counsel, which was still thankfully pro bono. The lawyer I was assigned said that I was not the first person that she had defended in a case against Gina.

I spent four months in jail, thinking Gina would drop the charges and that she wouldn't show up to court. But she did and she was persistent. The former DA had been on my side, but then there was a brand new one who believed Gina. She can be as convincing as the devil. She convinced Terry to marry her so as not to testify against her. It hurt to think the man who loved me was betraying me. But I could see clearly now that this was just a game to control me. Over two years, they had made at least $100,000 off of my work. Eventually, I decided not to fight the case because I was facing 15 years in prison if I lost.

Before I did that, I knew I needed help. I was in Orange County Jail which is one of the biggest jails in the country; nearly 400 women are there on a daily basis. My dorm was a substance abuse program jail with a state certified substance abuse recovery program. 5 days a week, 7 hours a day, we would do treatment programs: AA meetings, group meetings, devotions in the mornings, various curriculums, and other activities. Eventually I graduated and became a big sister of the program. They allowed me to start facilitating daily activities.

Residents Encounter Christ is a retreat program that they would bring into the jail for residents who were in a dorm. Something about the experience deeply affected me. I realized that I had believed that there was a God, but I had never asked him for anything that was about His will. I always just wanted his help. I had a moment when I was sitting in the rec yard after the retreat, and for the first time in my life I was honest with myself and with God. I said, "I can't anymore." And I meant it. I wasn't saying it to fool myself or anyone else. But because I really couldn't continue life like I had anymore. I was terrified, but I was giving up my pride, my addiction, everything I'd ever known. I was asking for help into a new way of life. It terrified me, but I felt a weight lifted off my shoulders; I felt peace. I gave my heart to Jesus. I said, "I don't know what this looks like. I don't know who You are. I don't even know who I am or what I'm doing. But

I want more of whatever I just felt. I now want to spend the rest of my life for You."

In addition to REC, Inside Out Jail Ministry that also really impacted me. They help you get into a program of recovery if you graduate their program first, to show you're committed. I went to all three classes. In one meeting, our leader asked us for the number one reason for failure in a recovery program. Our group guessed that friends, peer pressure, drugs, etc were factors. She said yes those are all true, but it's really authority. The number one reason for failure is that we don't want to listen to authority. That resonated with me, because the only time I listened to somebody else was when there was a threat. I remember it as early as my relationship with my stepfather... he used to tell me that if I told anybody anything he would kill me and my friends.

So once I graduated from Inside Out Jail Ministry, I got a mentor. She secured a couple of interviews for me with some programs. One of my stipulations for a program was that I could smoke cigarettes, and that eliminated a lot of recovery programs. I prayed about it and was in an AA meeting surrounded by like-minded people. There, someone told me about The WellHouse and how it was created for women who had been trafficked. I said that I wasn't really trafficked because I chose to do those things myself. I believed that. I still struggle with it from time to time, but I knew I needed to get into a program. I interviewed with the intake person at The WellHouse, and she asked a couple of questions:

"Have you worked for somebody, have you been sold, etc?"

'Yes, I definitely have." Then I confessed to her that I had a violent felony aggravated assault. I didn't know if the charge would stick but I had it, and they had to discuss it with the board. They agreed to let me in... by the grace of God!

I was offered 5 years of probation for my charges, including the time that I was at The WellHouse. I check in once a month, and it is a good reminder of the life I used to live, the life where God found me and redeemed me. I have been sober for 2 years. God is good and continues to amaze me with the way He loves me.

School and work are going well, and I even made the President's List. I officially have partial custody of my daughter. I have a choice in what I allow to upset me and what I don't. I am learning more about the way God sees me. With his spirit and power, I can love others the way God loves me.

God has given me purpose for my suffering, and I want to share it. And I want to help other women who have been through similar trials to heal, too. Because I can testify first hand: *there is hope.* ◈

A PART OF OUR PROCESS

*G*RADUATION.

Finally, the day of completion arrives, and she graduates! Graduation is one of the most beautiful things that happens at The WellHouse.

Surrounded by her new friends, her mentor, The WellHouse staff, and sometimes her family from home, she is celebrated at a ceremony in our chapel followed by an all-campus lunch. This is a holy and precious time.

Countless goals have been reached and she is ready to transition to independent living in the apartments, which she had her sights set on since she arrived.

She is thriving.

ESTHER

"Fear not, for I have redeemed you;
   I have called you by name, you are mine.
When you pass through the waters, I will be with you;
   and through the rivers, they shall not overwhelm you;
when you walk through fire you shall not be burned,
   and the flame shall not consume you.
For I am the Lord your God,
   the Holy One of Israel, your Savior.

                                        –Isaiah 43:1–21

had never had a panic attack like when I was in the holding cell before testifying on the stand against two of the biggest prostitution kingpins in Miami.

Whether or not to testify was a hard decision to make. I wasn't a snitch, but I felt like it was my ticket out of the life I had been living. I knew that if I did this, I couldn't go back to the streets. I wanted to actually change. I needed to start over.

I called my dad by his first name. My mom would get onto me, saying that I needed to call him "dad," but he was in and out of prison. He had a lot of DUIs and refusals to pay child support.

So it was just me and mom growing up. She was a taxi driver in Miami. Thankfully, she had a lot of help from her sister who lived nearby us, because my mom did a lot of hardcore drugs while I was growing up. Oftentimes, I felt like the mother in the relationship. My aunt had gotten clean when I was a baby, so she was really supportive when times got tough. She helped with babysitting or money or whatever was needed.

I didn't become rooted, because we moved a lot. I remember all the apartments, houses, and street names, like the rat house on Carpenter Street.

At one point, DCS stepped in because my mom was on drugs. Somehow they caught wind. But we just moved again. My mom would leave for days at a time and I wouldn't know where she was.

I remember that my mom started entering into sobriety programs and sticking with it, but then I started drinking. When she finally changed her ways, it was hard for me to accept that she was the one to make decisions now. So as a teenager, I was in the party scene.

My mom got really sick with MRSA so my aunt stepped up to the plate even more. She had a nurse aid come to change her sheets and assist with medications. Around that time, I began to experiment with drugs.

I met a lady next door named Stephanie. And this is probably where the real corruption began in my life. She had a little toy poodle just like mine, named Missy. That poodle was like my teddy bear at night when my mom was gone. She was a source of comfort.

But when I started hanging out with Stephanie, I would smoke weed with her. One night she asked me to leave, but I just wanted to keep smoking. So she said: "Okay. But I need you to not say nothing when you see what happens here." Her boyfriend comes over and gives her some dope. I was immediately hooked. I wanted more, but in order for me to get more, I had to perform sexual acts.

I didn't even know what was going on. All I knew was that I trusted my neighbor, Stephanie. I believed everything she said because she was cool. She got pills, like oxy. She had me selling them at school. For every one I sold at school, I could have one for myself.

My mom worked a lot. She would ask me about my days, but she had long and exhausting shifts. I told her it was none of her business. She would ask me why I was spending so much time at Stephanie's house. She knew I was smoking weed, but she still doesn't know that I was smoking crack over there at 14 years old.

By that time, I had already given myself away sexually.

Since we weren't the richest, it wasn't no big deal if I was walking down the street and an old guy said: "Hey, do you want to get in my car?" And he would pay me to get in his car. I was only 15 or 16.

I lacked meaningful friendships in my life and I began skipping school a lot.

My mom would drive to this park-and-ride place. I started hiding in her trunk after I made a copy of her key at a hardware store. She would park and head off on the bus to downtown, and I would pop through the back seat from the trunk into her car. I would take her car around to get pills, do drives for Stephanie, and take "friends" for rides to the mall. They were paying me gas and I was getting high.

It was probably a whole school year that I did that every day. My mom worked so much that she wasn't able to keep tabs on me. I changed the documents at school so that they called my phone instead of my mom. But as soon as I turned 16, I withdrew myself from school.

I finally got caught skipping school for an entire year. My family was so upset about it. My plan was to enroll in college after getting my GED. That didn't end up happening. When I was 17, my dad passed away. I got his survivor's benefits through social security. I felt like a grown up and like I didn't even need a job. I moved out of my mom's house when I was 18 and into my best friend's house.

This is when my life took a huge turn.

We had a party and I was arrested on my first charge ever: battery on a LEO[8]. I was released on my own recognizance and then was on probation living with my mom again.

---

[8] LEO: Law Enforcement Officer

I started meeting up with old friends that I had known when I was younger. I began doing middle man things, so I was drinking a lot and I was still getting by with the bare minimum to pass my drug test on probation. Pills stay in your system for 5 days. But I wouldn't do weed because that stays in your system for 30 days.

I met Braden. He didn't become my trafficker until after he found out that I had already been trafficked. But after a few months, he went to jail. His mom had brain cancer. She got 340 blues[9] a month. She was very addicted, but she was giving me some so I would go find more since she ran out before her prescription could be refilled. So we had a deal behind his back. She began to beg me to help her with the severe withdrawals since she did so many pills in a day.

One day I was riding on the bus crying. This girl sees that I am upset and begins to talk to me.

She learned about my financial woes and had a solution for me to get money. So at 19 years old, she took me to a hotel where I met my pimp, named Honest.

The lifestyle was glorified with purses, cars, nice things, but it was a raw deal. Honest was known as a gorilla pimp, which meant that he violently forced work and quotas. However many dates you did according to your phone messages, he would add up the amounts. If there was any money missing at the end of the night or if quotas weren't met, then you got a whooping. He would say: "I am very Honest to you. I give you this and I give you that." But Honest knew where you were at all times. You couldn't sneak a date, so I would just cuff tips. Although sometimes, he would go out drinking and I may be able to sneak one date and get the money for myself.

But I was terrified to leave or lead them to my family's house. I knew of one person who would protect me, Braden, but he was in jail. Through a mutual friend, he found

---

[9] Oxycontin

out that I had been tricking[10]. He was livid, but he knew the money was good. So when he got out of jail, he wanted a piece of the pie. I ended up cuffing money to leave Honest and did a midnight move.

Braden and I each owed a lot of money to drug dealers, so we decided to prostitute for a time. But this is when our relationship got rocky. He would be listening in the room nearby. I would tell him to go somewhere else.

Then I got caught in my first prostitution sting in 2011.

I was arrested at a hotel. There wasn't a lot of awareness then, so the cops kind of treated you poorly. They were rude and asked if I had someone outside waiting. They threatened me with a human-trafficking charge. I didn't really understand it. I ended up getting a slap on the wrist since it was my first time ever getting caught. I now had a $700 fine. I had a choice to make minimum wage or to make $800 in a day.

I chose to go back to $800 a day. I was able to get back my license that they had suspended by paying the fine through prostituting. We were driving all over to the city to convention centers and amusement parks so I could meet people for dates. I had so many dates that we started to miss some of them, so we began doing in-calls to our house.

He began controlling my online presence and profiles and I would just answer the phone for dates. I kept noticing these headlights across the streets from our house. I told Braden that I thought someone was watching us, but he said I was being paranoid since I was on coke. Soon our house was raided and I had drugs in the house. Braden escaped out the back and was able to post my bail, even though I was charged with prostitution.

I became more careful and worked at a strip club. I wouldn't prostitute unless I had seen the guy there for awhile and knew he wasn't a cop. Soon I was introduced to heroin

---

[10] Commiting an act of prostitution

and everything came to a crashing halt. I learned how to use the needles. Braden hated it and forced me to go into detox. I told the hospital that I wanted to kill myself if I couldn't get high, so they booked me into the psych ward. Braden got me out, and I felt like we would live happily ever after. But then he forced me back into the work.

I didn't want to do it unless I was numbed by drugs. I told him he lost his mind if he wants me to work sober. I couldn't keep up with my habit. I had a $300 per day habit at least. Plus other living expenses, it became too much and I went back to tricking.

I thought that I could do it alone. My mom was working in downtown Miami as well, so I was literally tricking down the street from where my mom was working.

I met these two guys and they wanted to pay me in heroin. I loved heroin at the time. They took me to a guy named Marcelino, who I ended up testifying against in court.

I had a whole clientele. I had a whole list of dates on my phones that I would contact. I didn't have a car and I was doing dates all by myself. I was having to go long distances to get my drugs and dates. So when I met Marcelino, he put me in a house and supplied my drugs. All my dates would come to the house, my own house.

I didn't realize that he was one of the biggest kingpins in Miami until later on. He had over 20 girls. He would come over, but he never kept a quota like Honest did. He would just be like: "What do you got for me?"

He would lay out drugs and leave.

It was very convenient. I liked our deal at the time. It was minimal control. I could come and go as I pleased. I could visit my mom, who knew I was high, but she didn't know I was back at tricking. And she certainly didn't know the extent of it.

Marcelino was under a 2 year investigation. He ran the West side of Orlando. Papa Murphy ruled the East side. They were rivals because they ended up both liking this one chick, Josie, who was the plug of it all. She organized all these drug deals. But, they were caught up in an investigation because of Josie.

When I was arrested, I was the first arrest they made on the whole case after two years. It was a sting operation. They got more girls and more charges. There were 24 co-defendants with me. Girls started pouring into the jail. My charges were increased to conspiracy to engage in racketeering patterns and to racketeering.

They had to keep us all separate in isolation. I stayed in isolation for 3 months. That seclusion really started taking a toll on me. I had to have a doctor come see me while I was in there and put me on antidepressants.

I cried a lot. I slept a lot. They would let us out for an hour a day. I read a lot of books. They eventually moved me to another county jail. I was held in that jail until court for a year. It was such a big case that they kept putting off the court date.

I didn't agree to testify until 9 months in because I was too scared to talk.

Finally my lawyer broke it down for me: she said: "Is he putting money on your books? Who is giving money for your phone? He is on the run and you are stuck in here."

He didn't put any money on my books. It was my family who was taking care of me. My mom was eating hotdogs to save money so she could put money on the books so I could use the phone just so she could talk to me.

My lawyer talked me into agreeing to testify with the state. But I had to sign a plea form. They sent me through a program called Samaritan Village. It was my first program. The WellHouse would eventually be my fifth program.

When I got arrested, I was pissed. I wasn't done yet. I couldn't wait to get back out there.

They were a small program in a neighborhood house. As soon as I hit the streets and I got into that house, I was full of anxiety and depression. I ended up getting high and leaving. I was on the run for a week. The state attorney was a big advocate for me and was on this case.

She had 24 defendants. Some of them she sentenced to prison right away. Others she gave a chance. I was one of the ones she gave a chance. Even after I ran away and got high, she came to the jail and she said: "I don't know what it is that I see in you Melissa, but I see something." I didn't know either because I felt like I was at my wits end and that I couldn't do recovery.

I felt like I was never gonna complete recovery. But she issued me back into the same program. After 8 months, I got into an altercation with a girl and got kicked out and went back to jail. They had to keep me because I was supposed to testify. So I was sent to a program in Tennessee, but I got caught stealing some Tylenol PMs. I ended up getting a warrant out for my arrest. I wanted to run, but I knew that if I ran, I was just going to prolong the issue. I was never gonna take care of it. There was always gonna be something I was going to be running from.

I was sentenced to 57 months for racketeering. I wasn't sad or in shock, but relieved. At this point, I felt like I couldn't do a program and that I was never going to recover. So in a way, there was relief in that sentence. My mom was in the court. She was crying and begging. The lawyer said they could attempt to get a reduced sentence if I could testify.

A couple of weeks went by and my mom was falling apart because I was going to be going to prison for years. She talked to my lawyer and they wanted me to testify. I gave in and agreed.

I ended up testifying against Marcelino and Papa Murphy, two of the biggest kingpins in Miami. During that time, I experienced the most severe panic attack I've ever had while in the holding cell.

The first day I spent an hour on the stand. The second day I spent three hours in cross-examination. I had a huge advocate team in the stands there to support me, but some of the testimony I choked out, barely able to speak.

Choosing to testify was hard. I felt like it was my ticket out of the life I had been living. I knew that if I did this, I couldn't go back to the life I had been living. I wasn't a snitch, but I wanted to actually change.

Their lawyers tried to trip me up by saying that I copped a plea deal. But I said: "I was sentenced to 57 months and I didn't have to testify. But I decided to turn around and testify, because there needs to be awareness and this needs to be stopped."

Marcelino and Papa Murphy both got 25 years a piece. There is a huge part of me that wonders if I did the right thing...

After my testimony, my sentence was reduced and I was sent to another program. When that one didn't work out, the state said that I could choose a program.

I chose The WellHouse.

It was a lot different than the programs I had been to previously. This was much bigger. I was really happy to be there. I truly experienced a lot of grace.

I felt like a social butterfly. The girls were outside smoking two weeks after my arrival at The WellHouse and we started talking about wanting to get high.

Some of the girls from Birmingham decided to escape

out of a window. I was ambivalent about whether I wanted to leave. One of the girls knew my story and she said: "Well if you stay, are you just going to snitch on us like you did on your pimp?" That stung because I had been struggling with guilt about my testimony. So I went with them.

Our house mom came looking for us down the street. Some of the girls were kicked out. But for some reason, me and another girl from out of state were allowed to stay. I don't know what their reasoning was, but I felt like I was given a real chance.

From that point on, I felt like God had shown me so much grace. I changed and chose to submit to authority. That was always very hard for me, but this was something me and my counselor had been working on at The WellHouse. I had felt for so long that I didn't have a choice. And now God had told me: "The gates are open. You can go through those gates or you can stay. Nobody is forcing you to be here." And something just clicked for me. From then on my entire outlook changed on my participation in the program.

I was done complaining and all on board with my program.

I was given a mentor named Mrs. Cindy. When she came into the picture, not too long after jumping out of the window, I was driven by Mrs. Cindy to a doctor's appointment. I blabbed about all that had happened. She said: "Listen, this is going to be a safe place for you. You can tell me anything and everything and nothing will leave this car." It was the best feeling in the world to have someone so close when my family was so far away from me at the time. To have a tangible person near me who I could call and they would come get me, that I could go stay at her house, that really helped my path at The WellHouse.

Living with 10 women can be difficult sometimes. But, Mrs. Cindy has been a huge light to my time at The Well-

House. One of my house moms said: "Look at it this way, Melissa, look at it as a journey you are on. Each time you fail is not necessarily a mess up, it was just God bringing you to a new place, new people, new things to learn, new insights from each program."

This is when my heart opened up to God and my restoration and healing began. For so long I felt like I was never going to be anything other than a drug addict or a prostitute. But my view changed when I experienced so much grace and love.

So many blessings came my way. I paid off my fees to get my license back and I got a car. Before I graduated, I was able to get a job. Blessings came my way left and right. I truly felt that there was no condemnation for what I had done.

I kept getting caught smoking when I wasn't supposed to, and when you get in trouble you have to talk to Mrs. Marley. I was expecting to be shamed for my repeated offenses. But she said: "There is no condemnation. Why don't you try this: just keep waking up and trying." She didn't see someone who failed or someone who was going to keep failing. She just wanted me to keep trying. And because she saw someone who could try, I believed that I could do it.

My whole journey at The WellHouse was full of little nudges that got me to the next stage of healing.

Not too long after that I started working at making pottery with my hands. I was then able to start a full-time job making pottery. I got a raise and started moving up. I am in school now too. I feel independent and strong.

My dreams for the future include being a physical therapy assistant. I see myself succeeding in these college classes, and when I look back at how far I have come, it nudges me to keep going.

I want to work in a profession where I help other people. I want to offer a gentle touch and a kind heart. I want to help other people succeed in gaining mobility. I think it's cool that I could be the one to build them up and tell them it'll be okay.

And because God brought me to this place, I know it will be okay. ✧

A PART OF OUR PROCESS

*T*RANSITIONAL LIVING.

Transformation has taken place in every area of her life: spiritually, emotionally, physically, and mentally. Pathways in the brain have begun healing as she is no longer abused or forced to abuse substances, and the trauma has subsided.

Life in the Transitional Living apartments affords a Well-House graduate the opportunity to continue her journey in the safety of The WellHouse. While there is much more independence than previously, there is a safety net as she might not be quite ready to exit completely to independent living. The resident can count on ongoing support from The WellHouse here. She pays a nominal amount for rent, but this is saved for her and given back when she is ready to exit for true independent living thus allowing her to have deposits for utilities and rent toward sustainable and safe housing.

She is hardly recognizable from the moment she entered The WellHouse, except for those dreams that she came to believe could be hers.

And she has succeeded!

FAITH

Therefore, since we have been justified by faith, we have peace with God through our Lord Jesus Christ. Through him we have also obtained access by faith into this grace in which we stand, and we rejoice in hope of the glory of God. Not only that, but we rejoice in our sufferings, knowing that suffering produces endurance, and endurance produces character, and character produces hope, and hope does not put us to shame, because God's love has been poured into our hearts through the Holy Spirit who has been given to us.

Romans 5:1–11

It was a cult.

My parents were "missionaries," but their Gospel was not Good News and their God was not the God of the Bible. Even though biblical language was used in the teaching, incorrect interpretations of the Bible gave me a distorted view of God from an early age. For instance, I heard a lot about the love of God, but never about his justice. So, confusion from religion was the norm early in my life.

I considered myself a professing Christian, but it was a distorted theology. This type of incomplete and misinformed theology is responsible for creating false converts, causing people to believe they are saved by God, when they are still lost. I believe the Bible is applicable today and that I cannot change God's word to suit me. And most of all, I am glad that I now know the true God!

Fueling the distortion, I remember early on that my dad was abusive toward my mom. This was the first picture of what love looked like. My mom was broken but doing the best she could. After separating from my dad, she opened the door for dangerous people to enter our home. At age nine, I was inappropriately touched and molested by a woman. I felt too ashamed to say anything. Mom's boyfriends were also coming in and out. She had a sincere desire to help people, but this led to these dangerous people being in my life. These experiences put scars deep in my soul at a young age, and I began hating myself. I did not have much self-esteem to begin with, but these scars made it worse. The sexual trauma now became the lens in which I viewed my world.

It was instilled in my mind that the sexual acts were the only way to get attention and to have people love me. The emotions were too much to handle, and I was too immature to know how to deal with them appropriately. I began acting out in class at school due to the unresolved anger.

I met a 24-year-old guy when I was 16. He started sticking needles in my arms, and this was the first time I didn't have to be who I was. I felt normal from using the drugs. I felt relieved. I was finally okay. Initially, the drug use eased my anxiety and depression and gave me the ability to be around people and talk to people. But soon, it put me in high-risk situations with dangerous people.

I became an addict. Then I was trafficked at age 23 by my boyfriend, who became my daughter's father. He benefited off the sale of my body. I did it out of love thinking I was taking care of us, but the relationship did not work out as it became unbearable. After my boyfriend and I split up, I was on the streets and then in and out of jail for about 3 years. Much of that time I was prostituting myself.

When I was 28, I met a group of guys from the west side of Orlando. When they looked at me, they saw money. So, they offered me dope. They told me I owed them money, and I was forced to stay with them for 2 weeks.

This type of indentured servitude was another unexpected aspect of trafficking I had not experienced, a more evil side. I knew if I ran, they would come looking for me. But still, I decided to run after I paid off the debt they said I owed.

After running, I was in jail for a year. I had weaned off of drugs and felt like my body did not need them anymore, but, due to the unresolved trauma, I went back to using drugs and became dependent on them again. While my body had the opportunity to ditch the drug habit, I did not have the opportunity to truly heal by digging in and getting to the root of the reason for using drugs.

I was ripping and running the streets. I had numerous overdoses and stayed in the hospital. One guy wanted to take care of me. I was an attractive woman, and in his mind, he knew he could make money off me. He took care of me, but not in a good way. I got a blood infection and had horrible sores—another side effect of the drugs and trafficking and not having access to medical care. But he would not let me go to the hospital. He was buying antibiotics off the street. The sickness made it so he could not sell me, so he beat me. I felt he was my only source of survival by providing food, shelter, and drugs. I was too weak and too beaten up to leave. The psychological manipulation was the worst aspect of the situation. When the infection got bad enough, he let me go to the hospital. I was admitted into the hospital for weeks to clear up the infection, they kept me on pain meds to deal with the pain from the infection. By the time I was released, which was almost a month later, I was still addicted but able to steer clear from that trafficker.

I soon met another trafficker – Papa Murphy. One of his girls recruited me. He found himself in the middle of an investigation as the leader of a drug and human trafficking ring. I needed a place to stay, I couldn't keep a roof over my head, I was losing my clothes, I truly had nothing. They interviewed me and I was welcomed to their team not really knowing what it meant. But when Papa Murphy asked for my legal name, it was not a good sign.

The longer I stayed the more evil and more abusive Papa Murphy became. One of the girls had upset him by shorting him money, and she was beaten so badly that her back was black and blue. He made me and another girl go work out of a hotel. I complied, because I was terrified of him.

147

The only thing that loved me and that I loved was my dog. But when Papa Murphy tried to kill my dog, that was all I could take. So, I waited until he left the house, packed my things, and left. Soon after, law enforcement raided his house and arrested everyone.

By this time, I had been in and out of trafficking for a decade. There were whole portions of my past that I didn't remember until later on, like blank spots in my memory. But, with the arrest of Papa Murphy and everyone at the house, Law Enforcement was looking for me too; I was all over the news. I was eventually arrested and was offered a program. This is how I was introduced to The WellHouse.

A part of me wanted it, but there was a part that didn't want to let it all go. As toxic and sick as my lifestyle had become, I was not ready. There were parts that I was holding on to. I agreed to a plea deal which meant I had to complete a program and testify against my trafficker. I would go to jail for six years unless I abided by these conditions.

I came to The WellHouse, but when I went home on a pass for Thanksgiving, I used heroin and did not return. I was on the run for 42 days, before being found.

Strangely, the 18 years in active addiction and human trafficking were not as bad as the 42 days that I was back out using drugs again and being trafficked. Those 42 days were worse because I knew deep down that I did not have to live that way. I saw everything differently. Each encounter I had while back in that life was different. It was like I was finally seeing this world for what it was: evil.

Just being in this life again, the feeling was different. I saw everyone for who they really were. I could feel that we were doing the Enemy's work. This time was different because I had the Holy Spirit. I knew deep down that I was sinning and doing the wrong things. I felt so convicted. Yes, I had been regenerated, but I was just a baby in Christ. A seed had been planted at The WellHouse. It had not hit me that salvation was eternal; I was wanting to be saved from that moment. I was miserable. Originally, I had zero remorse for my actions, but now I was weeping over them. The old and new were at war.

I was on the run living in hotels, being trafficked, and being provided drugs. I could not hide anymore. I was hopping from drug house to drug house.

Someone called the police, I was arrested, and I went to jail. Oddly enough, I was relieved. I didn't have to run anymore. Even though I was very dope sick, it was okay after the initial detox. Soon, I started to read my Bible and I prayed. I didn't understand the depth of these actions, but I could not get enough. It was feeding the empty hole, speaking to my deep soul scars. God was consuming my thoughts. He was chasing after me!

The impending sentence was on me, and the State prosecutor did not want to come off the sentence. I felt they wanted to make an example of me, so they sentenced me to prison. I do not know how I knew, but I had this idea in my mind that I was not going to do all this time. My charges included racketeering, which basically means that I was acting as an enterprise to obtain money illegally. Prison is entirely different from county jail; drugs were readily available. Yet, I held onto my faith, onto my Bible, and onto prayer, and I did not use. I believed. I have no idea no idea how, but I still believed I would not serve all that time.

I worked on myself. Even though I was still unwell, sick, and broken, I knew if I could not stay clean in prison, then I could not do it outside of prison. I stuck to it and stayed clean from drugs for 14 months.

There was an appeal for my sentence. As I was talking to a law clerk, another clerk heard me, came up to me, and said she needed to talk. She told me about an attorney who takes cases pro bono if the crime was a direct result of trafficking. She gave me the paperwork. I took it back to my cell and later called Tammy Spence who has a ministry to prisons and jails, and she said she met an attorney who works to get people out who were sentenced due to trafficking. It was the same attorney! She gave me the address for him. I had already hired an attorney for my appeal. By the time I completed the paperwork and had a conference with the trafficking attorney, there was a new prosecutor.

There was no one to testify against Papa Murphy; they had no reliable witnesses at the time. So, the attorney talked to the prosecutor, and they were going to bring me in for the trial. One attorney was going after expungement and the hired attorney was going to get a new plea deal to lessen the sentence. Oddly, there was another soon to be WellHouse resident who received the same deal as we had the same trafficker! At this point, I did not care if they only took six months off my sentence. Papa Murphy deserved to be in prison for the rest of his life, so I testified against him. He received 25 years! Afterwards, they completely dropped my charges and vacated my sentence.

But, what now? I still needed help. I contacted Tammy Spence who helped me get to Her Song.

I came to Her Song determined because this time, I wanted it so badly. I resolved to do whatever it took. I was not court ordered, but I had had a small taste of a different life. It was hard. The first nine months were the hardest. I was re-learning everything and rehashing the trauma, all while clean and without drugs to distract me. I couldn't see past the moment or pain I was in at that time, I wanted to give up, but the staff said "no, not today." They surrounded me and showed me the love of Christ.

The side effects of what I endured from childhood include complex trauma which is similar to PTSD, deeply affecting the brain and body. I struggle with being an intro-vert, and I still have fear and severe anxiety from living on high alert, constantly in a fight or flight mode. While it is amazing what the body and mind can do, how does one turn it off after leaving the life? Sometimes I will forget to breathe, and the anxiety is almost debilitating. But Christ gets me through it, and I keep moving forward.

I feel so humbled because of the wretched sinner I am, and yet, God hand-picked me! I've worked very hard for ev-erything, but the true blessing is God's grace and mercy.

I decided to go to college to pursue a career. I studied law. I got a job, and even though it was not what I wanted, I needed the experience. I saved for a car, and I resolved the issues with my license. I was the first one in that pro-gram to become a pioneer in speaking for them. I came to a point where I had completed everything they required, but I needed something more. I moved to the Beach House which was their transitional living house. All-in-all, I was in the program for 2.5 years. I even saved $20,000, and I wanted to buy a house. I stayed until I was ready, careful not to leave too soon. And I eventually bought my first house – on my own.

Today, I am so very honored to be working alongside Her Song, a ministry of the Tim Tebow Foundation.

While my time at The WellHouse was brief compared to Her Song, at The WellHouse, I was shown that I did not have to live this way anymore. I was shown that I was loved, val-ued, worth so much more. The WellHouse shared the Gospel with me, and that made all the difference!

If I could say anything to someone in a similar place where I was, it would be this:

It's not by chance you are where you're at. I know the road has been long and it has been rough. I know that some days you don't feel like you can make it another second, but something has brought you to this very moment and has sustained you to be here. You were made for more, you are beautiful, you are worthy, and you are loved. Please don't give up. Keep fighting for yourself. God can turn your pain into triumph and make beauty from ashes. There will be a moment where you will look back and say, "I am no longer the person I never wanted to be."

Just have a little faith.
Stay.
Fight.
No matter what. ✧

A PART OF OUR PROCESS

A NEW LIFE
Completing these final steps of the journey through The WellHouse leaves a formally traumatized, hopeless survivor of human trafficking with confidence and self-esteem and hope that her faith in God will lead her to continued success.

Those who choose to maintain contact with The WellHouse after their final exit often offer to share their stories, and, without exception, their gratitude includes the opportunity to have accepted and grown in faith.

Faith sustains her, guides her, and ensures that she will always be kept in the care of a God who loves her unconditionally.

The WellHouse is privileged to have had an impact that will last for eternity.

DEBBIE

A WELLHOUSE STAFF MEMBER

They said to the woman, "We no longer believe just because of what you said; now we have heard for ourselves and we know that this man really is the Savior of the world."

- John 4:42

It was just another Tuesday. I gathered my thoughts and my things and slipped quietly out the door. On the edge of town was a place where I could have a drink without the gaze of my disapproving neighbors. I let myself in and took a seat.

Before long, the bells on the entrance door jingled and a man I had (thankfully) never seen before walked in. He had the look of a traveler, weary and weathered. I turned back to my drink and was one sip in when he spoke. "Can you help me get a glass of water?"

Halfway into the awkward silence I realized that he was talking to me. This was startling because most people do not speak to me, most people move to the other side of the room when I walk in. I've seen more than a few mothers shew their children away from me. I must be abhorrent to them; I'm unwelcome. Apparently, I'm also ungrateful and ill-willed because I don't want their counsel, nor do I care for their pity.

So, I answered in keeping with my "stellar" reputation. "You don't want to talk to me. The last thing you need is my help."

But he persisted, and to his credit, he seemed unphased. "If you knew the gift of God," he said, "And who it is that asks you for a drink, you would have asked him and he would have given you living water."

I turned. He continued, "Everyone who drinks this water will be thirsty again, but whoever drinks the water I give them will never thirst. Indeed, the water I give them will become in them a spring of water welling up to eternal life."

Exhale. "I think I'll have some of that."

It turns out, Living Water saved my life.

In the Bible, the fourth chapter of John, introduces us to this world famous woman at the well. The longer I serve at The WellHouse, the more alive her story becomes to me. I see her, strong and determined, but also isolated and wounded. I see Jesus too, but he doesn't carry another list of demands. He's not another tyrant. He's a traveler. He sits beside her and they drink water. He listens.

In Scripture, the woman said, "I know that the Messiah, called Christ, is coming. When he comes, he will explain everything to us." Then Jesus declared, "I, the one speaking to you – I am He."

In the book of John, the woman at the well was the very first person to whom Jesus revealed his identity. Why was this? Was Jesus making a statement? Was he trying to teach us that every person that has ever walked this earth, even you, even me (and even she) is in desperate need of a listening ear?

Maybe. But The WellHouse challenges me to think bigger.

What I think is that it was love. Jesus loved the woman at the well as much as he deeply, profoundly, tirelessly loves the women at The WellHouse.

Throughout the ministry of Jesus, we see that He drew near to the downcast, the overlooked, the broken, the poor, and the heavy-laden. He spent his time with sinners of the lowest earthly status. He ate and drank with them. He healed them. He washed their feet. And ultimately, He demonstrated his love by willingingly dying for them, subjecting his body to brutality of the worst kind out of his deep love for the world.

These stories from The WellHouse are a testament to that love that **rescues, restores, reframes, regenerates, and reignites.**

And his love has done so for the women you now know.

May you boldly share their stories and embody that love. May you stubbornly insist that with God, anything is possible, life is eternal, and that evil can and will be overcome.

Jesus has overcome! And because of Him, we can know:

She is safe.

---

[11] This imagined retelling is inspired by the story of the woman at the well found in John 4.

THE WELLHOUSE
What We Do

RESCUE AND RESPOND

+ Rescue through our 24-hour crisis call line
+ Partner with FBI, Homeland Security, and local law enforcement to respond to crisis calls
+ Accept referrals from street outreach partners, hospitals, shelters, and more

SHELTER & STABILIZE

+ Provide emergency shelter and stabilization in our Trauma Center
+ Administer complete medical and daily therapy
+ Welcome victims into a retreat of calm, safety, and rest

HEAL & RECOVER

+ Shelter survivors for up to 4 months in our short-term home, The Immediate Shelter
+ Provide food, clothing, and medical care
+ Assist in regaining identification
+ Offer individual and group therapy opportunities for spiritual growth, substance abuse recovery, art therapy, work therapy, and equine therapy
+ Facilitate community relationship building and bonding with others

RESTORE & EQUIP

+ Accommodate survivors for up to 12 months in our long-term program, Next Steps to Freedom
+ Equip with job skills and employability
+ Assist with educational goals (like GED & college)
+ Provide transportation and help obtain vehicles
+ Offer life skills classes including financial literacy, cooking, group exercise, and more
+ Continue all therapy programs

STRENGTHEN & PROPEL

+ Supply graduates with a transitional living program, Next Steps to Independence
+ Secure graduates in full-time employment
+ Help to find safe, sustainable, permanent housing for graduates after exiting
+ Offer ongoing counseling and case management

RESOURCE

Human Trafficking Facts

+ Human trafficking has occurred if a person was induced to perform labor or a commercial sex act through force, fraud, or coercion. Minors age 19 and under engaging in commercial sex are considered to be victims of human trafficking, regardless of the use of force, fraud, or coercion.

+ The United States was ranked one of the world's worst places for human trafficking in 2018.

+ 83% of sex trafficking victims in the US are US Citizens.

+ 80% of victims are female, and up to 50% are minors.

+ Ages 12–17 are the most common age of entry.

+ Quotas are estimated to be between $200-$1,000 per girl; all money is kept by the trafficker.

+ Victims are punished terribly, starved or beaten, if they do not meet their quota.

+ Traffickers can make $150,000-$200,000 per girl per year; the average trafficker handles 4-6 girls.

+ An estimated 1.5 million children run away from home each year; it is common for those children to be recruited into sex trafficking.

+ Human trafficking is estimated to be a $150 billion industry.

RESOURCE
Human Trafficking FAQs

Q: What is the difference between human trafficking and prostitution?

A: The difference is whether the person in question is self-promoting. Human trafficking occurs when there is a pimp or trafficker using force, fraud, or coercion to control their victim. Without these main factors, the crime is considered prostitution.

Q: Does human sex trafficking really happen in the United States or Alabama?

A: Human trafficking can happen anywhere. It is estimated that between 18,000 and 20,000 victims are trafficked into the United States every year. The United States, along with Mexico and the Philippines, was ranked one of the world's worst places for human trafficking in 2018. In addition, Birmingham has been identified as one of six major hubs in the South for human trafficking. Interstate 20 is known as the "Sex Trafficking Super-Highway." It is believed there are more trafficking victims that travel this stretch of interstate than any other stretch of interstate in the entire nation.

Q: **How profitable is the human trafficking industry?**

A: Human trafficking is an estimated $150 billion industry, making it the world's second largest criminal enterprise, second only to drug trafficking. Commercial sex is estimated to be a $110 million industry in the Birmingham metropolitan area. That does not include child sex trafficking or illegal massage parlors.

Q: **Are females the only victims of human sex trafficking?**

A: There is no single victim profile. Victims of human sex trafficking can be male, female, young, and old. They can also be from a variety of different socioeconomic backgrounds. However, victims of human sex trafficking specifically tend to be females. The International Labour Organization estimates that 99 percent of human sex trafficking victims were female in 2016.

Q: **Why would a victim choose to stay with their trafficker or choose not to seek help?**

A: There are many reasons why a victim might choose to remain in their situation, even if they are not physically being held against their will. For many, the bondage of a woman or girl to their trafficker is unseen. Traffickers might threaten their victims' life, children, or family. In other cases, the woman or girl being trafficked has come to rely on their trafficker financially for food, shelter, clothes, drugs, or transportation. Lastly, many victims of sex trafficking have endured enormous amounts of emotional manipulation and mental abuse. Victims believe they are truly trapped with no escape or that no one cares for them, other than their trafficker.

Q: Do victims ever relapse after they have been rescued?

A: Yes. Survivors may return for many reasons. Some lack the resources needed to be self-sufficient (i.e. job, money, shelter, transportation, etc.). Some victims have serious physical and mental health issues and have no support system. Once rescued, victims need to enter an immediate treatment facility to reduce the chances of relapse.

Q: Could my children be victims of trafficking and I not be aware?

A: Yes. Unfortunately, there are many cases in which children are victims of sex trafficking without the parent(s) ever becoming aware. To reduce the risk of your child becoming a target to traffickers, be sure to monitor their online activity, know exactly who your kids are with, and know where they are. Be open and understanding when talking with your kids about sex, relationships, and boundaries.

Q: Where are The WellHouse residents from, and how do they get to The WellHouse?

A: The WellHouse rescues victims from all over the U.S. and abroad, with a concentration in the Southeastern United States. In 2019, 45 percent of our residents were from Alabama. We receive trafficked victims by one of three ways:

- rescue through our 24-hour crisis call line
- partnership with the FBI, Homeland Security, and local law enforcement
- referrals from street outreach partners, hospitals, shelters, and more

Q: Do traffickers ever look for women and girls at The WellHouse Campus?

A: There has only been one instance of a trafficker pursuing a WellHouse resident. To prevent this from happening again, we only disclose our location with trusted staff and volunteers to ensure the safety of our residents. Traffickers, unfortunately, view those that "work" for them as commodities or objects. When they lose a woman or girl to law enforcement, rehabilitation services, etc., it is easier and cheaper for the trafficker to simply replace the woman with another.

Q: What should I do if I suspect trafficking is occurring to me, someone I know, or in my area?

A: If you think that you or someone you know may be a victim of trafficking, or if you see anything suspicious in your area, contact The WellHouse Crisis Line. We will be able to give you advice on what to do and potential next steps. Additionally, you can contact the National Human Trafficking Hotline at (888) 373-7888. If someone is in need of urgent assistance, contact your local police or dial 9-1-1.

---

* The above information was gathered from various sources including The WellHouse, Business Insider, U.S. Department of State, Department of Homeland Security, International Labour Organization, and Nationwide Children's Hospital.

RESOURCE

Human Trafficking Myths vs Facts

Myth: *Traffickers are only men.*

FACT: Traffickers can be both men and women. On a fairly regular basis, it happens that women who have been sexually exploited first, later join the criminal partnership and start to exploit other women themselves. Women are often involved in the recruitment process because they are seen as more trustworthy.

Myth: *Victims are only young girls.*

FACT: There is no single victim profile. Victims of human trafficking can be male, female, young and old. They can also be from a variety of different socioeconomic backgrounds. However, children are most vulnerable to traffickers.

Myth: *Traffickers target victims they do not know.*

FACT: Many victims of human trafficking are trafficked by family members, romantic partners, and friends.

Myth: *Traffickers only use drugs to keep their victims captive.*

FACT: Traffickers do use drugs to control their victims, but they also use other tactics such as physical and emotional abuse, isolation from friends and family, and economic abuse.

Myth: *People have to be kidnapped in order to be trafficked.*

FACT*:* Less than 1 percent of people who are kidnapped are actually kidnapped for the purposes of human trafficking, being sold into sex trafficking here in the U.S. Many traffickers use methods of manipulation, defrauding, or threatening behavior to force victims into providing commercial sex or exploitative labor.

Myth: *Human trafficking only happens in illegal or underground industries.*

FACT: Human trafficking cases have been reported in industries like restaurants, cleaning services, construction, and factories.

Myth: *Human trafficking mainly happens outside the United States.*

FACT: The United States has extremely high rates of sex trafficking. Large events in the United States, such as the Super Bowl and the Kentucky Derby, are among some of the top hotspots for sex trafficking.

Myth: *Victims will be easy to identify or they will self-identify.*

FACT: Every trafficking situation is unique and self-identification as a trafficking victim or survivor happens along a continuum. Fear, isolation, guilt, shame, misplaced loyalty, and expert manipulation are among the many factors that may keep a person from seeking help or identifying as a victim even if they are, in fact, being actively trafficked.

---

*Citation: Polaris Project. (2020, January 17). "Myths, Facts, and Statistics."

RESOURCE FOR LAW ENFORCEMENT
How to Spot & Report Human Trafficking

HOW TO IDENTIFY A VICTIM

+ Human trafficking has occurred if a person was induced to perform labor or a comercial sex act through force, fraud, or coercion. Minors age 19 and under engaging in commercial sex are considered to be victims of human trafficking, regardless of the use of force, fraud, or coercion.
+ 75% of victim recruitment occurs between 12-17 years old.
+ 90% of victims come from single parent homes and have documented abuse or neglect.
+ 96% of victims have been labeled as runaways.

WHAT TO DO WHEN ENCOUNTERING A VICTIM

+ If you come into contact with a suspected victim of human trafficking, first look at his or her charges. If the charges involve prostitution, drugs, trespassing, etc., these are clues that he/she may be experiencing sexual exploitation or human trafficking.

KEY QUESTIONS

+ Is anyone forcing you to prostitute?
+ Do you keep the money from the "clients" or does all, or a portion, go to another person?
+ Are you fearful for yourself or a family member if you reveal your situation?

KEY OBSERVATIONS

+ Signs of physical abuse: bruises, handprints, unusual marks
+ Tattoos or brandings (these signify ownership by another)
+ Nervousness, looking down, refusing to look you in the eye, anxiety, and fear
+ Victims often cannot self-identify. Due to trauma, their thoughts are jumbled, and his/her story will not always be clear or line up.

ONCE IDENTIFIED

+ Call **The WellHouse Crisis Line at 1.800.991.0948.**

THE WELLHOUSE
Want to Help?

JOIN US!

+ Spread the word. Buy this book for friends, or tell your circle what you learned from it and how The WellHouse helps women and girls.

+ Pray for The WellHouse residents, staff, volunteers, and board.

+ Learn more through The WellHouse Blog and Resources at www.the-wellhouse.org.

+ Shop handcrafted goods made by residents at The WellHouse in ShopWell here: the-wellhouse.org/store

+ Fulfill resident needs by giving items on our Needs List here: the-wellhouse.org/needs

+ Volunteer here: the-wellhouse.org/volunteer

+ Request a WellHouse speaker for your upcoming event here: the-wellhouse.org/contact

+ Support financially by donating here: the-wellhouse.org/donate-1relationship building and bonding with others

CONTACT US

Website: the-wellhouse.org
Email: info@the-wellhouse.org
Office Phone: 1.800.991.9937
Crisis Line: 1.800.991.0948
Mailing Address: PO Box 868, Odenville, AL 35120

A WORD OF THANKS

We would sincerely like to thank each of our volunteers, staff, donors, partners, and advocates who help make this ministry successful in serving survivors of human trafficking.

It is our hope that these stories of resilience and hope will encourage you as you give of your time, energy, talents, and gifts. It is our prayer that you will be blessed in your giving and that together we may see more captives set free, more chains loosed, and more dreams realized.

Thank you for your dedication and hard work.